Free Indeed

From Prison to Prosperity

By
Craig Nedrow

"If the Son makes you free, you shall be free indeed" (John 8:36).

"Beloved, I pray that you may prosper in all things and be in health, just as your soul prospers" (3 John 2).

XULOI
PRESS

D1416815

Acknowledgement

—ᴧᴧᴧ—

I would like to acknowledge and thank so many people that have helped get this book completed:

To Micah; thank you for your support and encouragement. There are sacrifices that you have made in support of God's kingdom work that are invaluable. Two are better than one; and you complete me more than you'll ever know this side of heaven. You truly are my better half in so many ways. I love you; thank you for suggesting over and over again for me to write about what God has done and continues to do.

To: Doug & Julie, Ethan, Stan G., Mark & Laura, John & Dustin @ Salem Communications, Casey & Nina, Terri & Jerry, Gary F., Jeremy & Stephanie, Jason & Tiffany, Pete & Nancy, Mike & Cristel, Marty & Melia, Jim & Christine, Ted & Bella, Mark & Erika, and our Pastor's Michael & Debbie Gamble; May God continue to bless and keep you all! Writing a book is quite an undertaking; and I couldn't have done it without the support of all of you.

To our family: thank you to my family for your forgiveness of the years that I was lost, and to

Micah's family for accepting me into the family without judgement. Your love and support in our ministry is so important to us!

To all supporters of Craig Nedrow Ministries (CNM): God bless you ALL! Micah and I want to be good stewards with what The Lord has entrusted to us. These are serious times we are living in, and there are so many people that need the love of Christ and need to hear the truth of His word proclaimed. Please continue to pray that God will use CNM for His kingdom purposes, and that He will bless those who read this book.

This book is dedicated to the memory of Don & Ione Nedrow, Craig's mom and dad, and Ron Baze, Micah's dad; who have gone ahead of us to be with The Lord. We miss you and look forward to seeing you again soon. God is so good!

May God Bless You All! In Jesus Name! Amen!

Introduction

—ɯ—

First and foremost, this is *not* a "self-help" book. The world is flooded with self-help books and yet the pharmaceutical companies can't produce anti-depression medication quickly enough. The problem, in my humble opinion, is that we can't fix ourselves or else we would do it. People have been trying to "fix" themselves for thousands of years unsuccessfully.

This is my story, which hopefully you will find to be parts of your story as well. As an evangelist, businessman, husband and a very concerned American; I have the privilege of interacting with people from all walks of life, all levels of society, all incomes and all different faiths and I see some common characteristics. People, as individuals, are suffering in many different ways. And America, as a nation is suffering in many different ways.

My story, which we'll get to later, is real; it's raw, and in many ways it's disturbing, but many of you will be able to relate to it.

When I talk about prison, I was in a "physical" prison, but there are many different types of prison. I talk to people every week who are "imprisoned" in pornography, drug addiction, alcohol addiction, anger, bitterness, hatred and many other types of bondage.

And when talking about "prosperity", there is financial prosperity, but I'm talking about a different kind of prosperity. This is a kind of prosperity that many people are clueless to, but that God wants us to know about. This is *so* much more than financial prosperity.

Why write this book?

Throughout the last ten years many people have said to me, "You need to write a book." I'm sure they meant well, but the thought of writing a book sounded to me like an overwhelming task and it still seems that way. The thought came to mind, "Who would want to read a book that I wrote?" There is something called "confirmation", which is when you hear the same thing over and over again until finally you say, "Ok Lord, I got it". So, after many people encouraging me and after the parent company of the radio station where I have a program telling me the same thing, I've come to the realization that I should have listened (again) to my wife Micah in the first place when she said, "You need to write a book."

In these pages I am going to pour my heart out to you about my concern for people who are searching for a peace that they don't seem to be able to find but that has been granted to me.

I'm also going to discuss my concern for a nation that I grew up in and love, but no longer recognize. A nation that has lost its way.

You may think that these are two completely different topics, but they really aren't. As a nation's people go... so goes a nation. If the people of a nation are suffering, then a nation suffers. If the people of a nation prosper, the nation prospers.

Let me state something at the outset of this book as clearly as possible. This book is *not* about something that I have done. It's not a self-promotion book. The word "I" has to be used when telling what the LORD has done in my life, but it makes me cringe. This book is all about *what Jesus Christ can do* in a person's life. If the LORD took someone like me and changed my life, then He can and will change anyone's life. The hope is that by reading these pages, you will come to a greater understanding of the power and love of God. That He is still changing lives and that He can take anybody that He chooses and do whatever He chooses with that person. Also, that you will come to an understanding that His ways are different from our ways. That we may not be able to comprehend what His purposes are at the time, but that if we will trust Him and allow Him to, He will do the work in us and change us in ways that we can't change ourselves.

The Lord took me and broke me behind the walls of prison. But He is a loving God and when He breaks us, He never leaves us like that. He begins the process of restoring us, refining us and transforming us into the image of His Son Jesus Christ. The process can be painful, but God always has our best in mind. This book is about that process...

This is your invitation... take this journey with me from "Prison to Prosperity".

"Lord, may You bless those who read this book. May you speak through these pages to those who need to hear from You, who need Your love, Your touch and who need Your peace, which surpasses all understanding. Heal those who need healing and open the minds of us all to comprehend Your love for us. Use this book for Your Kingdom purposes. We ask these things in Jesus's name. Amen."

Table of Contents

—ɯ—

PRISON SECTION

Chapter 1

Keeping It Real!

—ᴍ—

I am definitely a Type A personality. Whenever I have the opportunity to speak somewhere, I tell the audience that I don't "candy coat" the message. The reason for that is because with my past, it's difficult to smooth out the story. It would be great if I could tell you that I was a pastor's kid, raised in the church and never got into any trouble, but that would be a lie. I chose to walk a different path that was in many ways disturbing. We all have a past and while I'm not proud of mine, I have to share it. Until you get an understanding of how lost I was you can't fully appreciate how gracious God is and how amazing His transforming power can be in a person's life. When Jesus changes a person's life, the proper word to describe what that person has been through is the word "testimony". If you've been born again, then you have a testimony. It's the "before and after" story that the song *Amazing Grace* speaks about. "I was once lost, but now I'm found; I was blind, but now I see." It's your testimony...

"They overcame him (Satan) by the blood of the Lamb and the word of their testimony" (Revelation 12:11).

The word "testimony" in the Greek language is *martyra* and it means "witness" or "report". When we report to others what Jesus has done in our lives, that's witnessing. A witness tells the truth about what they have seen and they report what has happened. When we witness to others about what Jesus has done in our lives, it makes the Gospel real and the devil absolutely hates it. This book is my testimony about how Jesus Christ changed and is still changing my life. It's real, it's raw... and as I already mentioned, it's sometimes disturbing. The truth often is.

I was raised in Richardson Texas, a suburb of Dallas. The family I grew up in was a typical middle class American family. There was love; we weren't rich or poor. I was involved in sports, liked girls, had two sisters that I drove crazy and an older brother that I always looked up to. I made decent grades in school and by all indications I was headed in the "right" direction in life. I went to something called "Young Life" at church on Monday nights. If you would have asked me if I was saved, I would have said yes, but the truth is I didn't have a clue what that meant. I went to Young Life to check out the girls and the center of my life was sports and my friends. Sound familiar to anyone else out there?

I was so good at sports that many people, including myself, thought I would eventually be a pro athlete. When I got to college, I realized I wasn't good enough to be a pro athlete and there was a huge void in my life that I didn't know how to fill. In life I find there are those who have achieved their dreams and those who haven't, but a common denominator is the *"Is this all there is in life?"* feeling. When I reached that point, I began to make some poor choices. There are consequences for choices we make in life. When I speak to youth today, I always say... "If you don't hear anything else I say, hear this... who we run around with makes a huge difference in our lives."

The Bible says...

"Do not be deceived, evil company corrupts good habits" (1 Corinthians 15:33).

Think about this... how many times when someone we know begins to get into trouble and have problems, people who are close to that person will say, "I don't like the crowd that he or she is running with." The people we associate with are *very* important in life.

After college I came back to Dallas and got involved in the restaurant and nightclub scene. That was one of those poor choices that I'm talking about. I soon got involved in everything that went with that scene, including the drugs. I never sold drugs, so my thinking was that I wasn't hurting anyone else. What a selfish attitude, but that was how I felt. Everybody else around me was doing drugs, so what's the big deal, right?

That's the thing... we never stop to think about the consequences of our choices or who else our decisions may affect. Over the years of prison ministry that I've been involved in, I have seen firsthand the thousands upon thousands of families that have been destroyed by the drug use of one member of the family. It's devastating to witness and yet if those of us who have been drug addicts would have stopped and thought about our families, most of

17

us never would have gotten involved in that life. I repeat... there are consequences for our choices!

The choices that I was making would have a major effect on not only my life, but my parents, my brothers and sisters, the rest of our family, even my close friends that had known me for years.

Drug addicts are not able to think clearly because their minds have been chemically altered, so their decision-making becomes skewed. Usually, one bad choice after another begins to take place and that's what happened with me.

The next several years are what I refer to as the wandering years. I held different jobs and even pursued a career (which may be another book someday), but my life had no real purpose. When we go through life, it's easy for us to lose sight of what God really has planned for us.

"The thief does not come except to steal,
and to kill, and to destroy" (John 10:10).

I am a witness that the Devil is content when we wander through life without fulfilling God's purpose for our lives. Satan wants to steal years away from us; he wants to kill people's dreams they may have for their lives and he wants to destroy relationships. That's what he does and who he is. He's the enemy of our souls. For many years that is exactly what he did in my life. That's why I am able to recognize the same thing in other people's lives. But God is a redeemer who is well able to fulfill His purpose. We may not understand or like His purpose when we're going through something difficult. That brings me to the next part of my testimony...

I left a party one night and as I was walking to my truck in the parking lot, the Dallas Police stopped me. It was very late and they searched me because I was in the part of Dallas known as the club area. I didn't have any drugs on me, but they hit the remote of my car keys and decided to search my truck. They found two empty baggies with cocaine residue on them. I was arrested and charged with possession of a controlled substance.

Now at this point, let me be clear that what had just happened to me shouldn't have come as any great surprise. My family had tried to talk to me many times about my drug use. I had even been arrested a few times, but this was about to become much more serious. My brother, who lived out of state, came to Dallas and tried to find me for an intervention. One of my sisters was in a prayer group that prayed I would be arrested and sent to prison. My life at this point was obviously out of control. God sends us warning signs that we can either receive and listen to or reject and suffer the consequences. I chose to reject those warning signs and I was about to suffer the consequences.

I was now in Dallas County Jail. I went before the judge and the words that I was about to hear would change my life. The judge said to me, "Mr. Nedrow, you've landed in the wrong court on the wrong day; I am going to make an example of you. How do you plead?" I said "Not guilty," because that's what everybody says when they get arrested. The judge said, "I'm no bonding you." That means that you're not going to be allowed to bond out. Then the judge said, "Here is my offer to you: eight years in prison." *Eight years!* You could have knocked me over. I said, "I can't do eight years in prison." The judge then said, "Send him back to his cell." I was put in a cell with 23 other men. I spent the next month in that cell, called a "tank".

During that month, my mother sent me a Bible and I began to read it. After one month, the judge brought me back to court and dropped the offer to seven years. I said, "Your honor, I am begging you for probation." And she said, "I'm not offering you probation, Mr. Nedrow. You're going to prison." And I said, "I can't do seven years in prison." And she sent me back to my tank again. This went on for the next five months. Every month she called me back into court, lowered her offer by a year and I would say no. She would send me back to my tank for another month. After five months of this, she said, "This is my last offer... two years in prison, or go to trial. But, if we go to trial, I will win and you will lose and I will give you eight years in prison. Am I making myself clear on that?" And I said, "Yes, your honor." Then she told me I had one week to decide – go to trial or take the two years.

My mother came to visit me that week and asked me, "Are you innocent?" I said, "No, ma'am," and she told me to take the two year sentence because she couldn't live with the thought of losing me for eight years. Like so many men, I'm a momma's boy through and through and when I thought about the tremendous pain that I caused my mom, my family and friends, it devastated me. It took a long time for me to begin to forgive myself for the heartache that I caused so many of my family, friends and people who cared about me.

One of the tragedies of prison is that the families of inmates have to learn how to do the time the inmate has. I will discuss the prison experience in greater detail later in this book.

I went before the judge the next Friday and took the two year prison sentence. I was guilty as charged. In reality, many times I had been in possession of drugs and had *not* gotten caught. I'm fortunate that I never died from my drug use. I had been shot at, had guns pulled on me and could easily have been killed from the dangers that are associated with the drug world. And honestly, I deserved more time than I actually got sentenced to. I broke the law, got caught and I was on my way to prison.

But God had a plan. I mentioned that my mom sent me a Bible in jail, and I had started to read it. I had no idea what impact that would have on me. There is a verse that says...

> *"You meant evil against me, but God meant it for good" (Genesis 50:20).*

What the devil intends for evil, God can and does use for His good. We all love to hear about the blessings from God, but there's a flip side that needs to be talked about and that would be the correction from the Lord. Some people have said to me over the years, "The devil sent you to prison," but that's simply not the case. God's hand was involved in me going to the penitentiary. As I mentioned before, the devil was content when I was wasting my life using drugs and not living for the Lord.

> *"My son, do not despise the chastening of the Lord, nor detest His correction; for whom the Lord loves He corrects" (Proverbs 3:11, 12).*

I am a witness that sometimes we need the disciplining of the Lord. It's absolutely amazing what began happening after I was sentenced to prison. At this point I had been locked up for five months. When a person goes to prison in Texas, they first go to what is called an "ID" unit where it is determined where they will spend the majority of their time. The "ID" unit was called "Gurney" and there I was told that I had been chosen for an experimental program. The Texas Department of Corrections (TDC) had chosen 173 men in the state to enter into the first "Faith Based Program" in the state. We were sent to a small unit in east Texas where we had Bible studies seven days a week and church seven nights a week. In an average week, I was ministered to by six to ten different pastors. I began spending ten to twelve hours a day studying God's word and it literally changed my life! When I speak, I tell people that going to prison was the one of the greatest things that ever happened to me. What a crazy statement to make.

"Be still and know that I am God"
(Psalm 46:10).

This has become one of my "life scriptures". For me, it took going to prison to get still and to come to the realization that He is God. I believe that most people have never really stopped long enough to meditate on and understand this verse. We run so fast in this world today and when the storms in life come (and we all know they do come), our first inclination is to try to fix the problem ourselves. That often just makes the problem worse. Or we try to get out of the problem which usually just delays it until later. We try everything else first and then when we're at the end of our rope, we cry out for God to intervene.

What if we stopped, got still and sought the Lord before we did anything? What if we just stopped... said "Ok Lord, You know exactly what's going on here and I need You to direct my steps. I need Your wisdom here to know what to do. Are You wanting to show me something? Your will be done here, Lord. I am going to be still, because I know that You are God and You are in control." He may very well be trying to bring us to the place of surrender where we will trust Him instead of ourselves.

I spent a total of sixteen months locked up: five months in Dallas County and eleven months in prison. I look back on that time with fond memories because that's when I got born again and the Lord began the process of transforming my life.

"Bring my soul out of prison, that I may praise Your name" (Psalm 142:7).

Another "life verse" for me. I must tell people about Jesus Christ. After what He has done in my life, how can I not tell others about Him? While I was in prison, I told the Lord that any door He would open for me, I would be a bold witness and tell people about how He changed my life. I must praise His name!

I walked out of prison on January 2, 2002. Immediately the Lord began opening doors for me to testify about how He has changed my life. I've had the privilege of speaking in both secular and Christian schools, as well as many churches around the country. The Lord has opened doors for me in

Prison Ministry, Juvenile Ministry, Men's Ministry and I was invited to be the keynote speaker at the National Command Center of the Salvation Army in Washington D.C.

In October 2009 Micah and I felt led to start a ministry called "Stand Up 4 Jesus". This ministry is a call for Christians to stand up, speak out and contend for our Christian faith and rights in America. We held an event in July 2010 and several thousand people attended. From this event came a radio program, also called "Stand Up 4 Jesus". We have been on the air since March 2010. The parent company is Salem Communications, the largest Christian Broadcasting Company in America. The radio program has a listening area of several million people.

I have to tell you that by the world's standards none of this makes any sense for someone that came out of prison, but when the hand of the Lord is on a person all things are possible. I am sold out for Jesus! The Apostle Paul said...

> *"That I may speak boldly, as I ought to speak" (Ephesians 6:20).*

I pray the same for me; that the Holy Spirit will empower me to "speak boldly as I ought to speak." After what the Lord has done in my life, He deserves my very best. I have been given a gift with the Scriptures, to be able to understand, teach and apply the word of God in our daily lives. I believe every word in the Bible! It says...

> *"All Scripture is by inspiration of God, and is profitable for doctrine, for reproof,*

for correction, for instruction in righteousness, that the man of God may be complete, thoroughly equipped for every good work" (2 Timothy 3:16,17).

Notice it doesn't say 92%, or 97%, it says *"all"*. It also says by "inspiration" of God; that means "God breathed."

"Holy men of God spoke as they were moved by the Holy Spirit" (2 Peter 1:21).

The Bible *is* the word of God. Just because some people don't believe that, doesn't change that fact. There will be a day when each person will stand before God and then they can give their defense to God as to why they believed the Bible isn't His word. As for me, I choose to believe what He says.

"Heaven and earth will pass away, but My words will by no means pass away" (Matthew 24:35).

Jesus spoke those words and I choose to believe what Jesus said!

When I speak in prisons, churches and to youth groups, I tell them that I can come and preach to them, but if I don't give them a message that they can apply in their lives, then I really haven't helped them. God's word teaches us how to treat our spouses, how to raise our families, how to handle our finances and how to live our lives in a way that we can't do without His word.

I will never compromise the Scriptures. Many in this nation have turned away from the Lord. That can be debated, but it's the truth. We have grown lukewarm and we have not obeyed God's word. As a matter of fact, we as a nation have rebelled against the word of God. I will address these topics in great length in this book.

Now that you know some about my testimony, let's begin to go deeper...

Chapter 2

We've Been Lied To

—ɯ—

One of the *very* worst feelings in the world is being arrested, put in a jail cell and hearing that cell door clank shut. Ask anybody that has ever been locked up... whether for one day or 20 years and they will tell you that's a true statement.

With me, it represented that I couldn't talk my way out of the situation. The lies, the manipulation, the running – it was all over with and I had finally been caught. There is a feeling of panic that comes over you when you've been arrested. Even at this point, your mind races trying to figure a way out of the situation. Who can I call to get me out? What can I say that will make this sound like it's not my fault? This isn't fair that I am in this situation. I can't believe that I'm here.

Truth be told... I lied to my family, I lied to myself and I lied to God. It was all one big lie! The tragic part is that ...*we've all been lied to!*

Allow me to prove my point. The Bible says...

"The whole world lies under the sway of the wicked one" (1 John 5:19).

Notice it doesn't say "Omaha, Nebraska lies under the sway of the wicked one", or "Dallas, Texas lies under the sway of the wicked one". It says "the *whole world*". The word "lies" in that verse is a verb that means "to be appointed or destined to". The word "sway" means "govern or rule" or "under the control of". So that verse actually reads like this...

"The *whole world* is destined to be under control of the wicked one."

That may not be a popular thought, but look at the proof. With all the knowledge we have in this world, all the technology, all the love, all the resources, why can't we solve world hunger? Or disease? Why can't we live at peace with each other? Why is the world so violent? Why is there so much depravity in the world? Why is there so much corruption in the world? What about child abuse? Why all the evil? Because... "the whole world lies under the sway of the wicked one."

Let's talk about "the wicked one". This is important because we need to know who our enemy really is. He has a name. His name is Satan. He's the devil. He's real. And the sooner you and I realize that, the sooner we can begin to understand what we're up against and how to overcome Him. The very first thing that we must understand is that he's a liar. Listen closely to what Jesus said about him in John 8. The setting here was that Jesus was having a confrontation with the religious leaders (I will talk more about "religion" later.) They hated Jesus because he spoke the truth to them...

> *Why do you not understand My speech?*
> *Because you are not able to listen to My*
> *word. You are of your father the devil,*

28

and the desires of your father you want to do. He was a murderer from the beginning, and does not stand in the truth, because there is no truth in him. When he speaks a lie, he speaks from his own resources, for he is a liar and the father of it. But because I tell the truth, you do not believe Me. (John 8:43-45)

There it is... Satan, the devil, is a liar. As a matter of fact, he's the father of lies. And if "the whole world lies under the sway of the wicked one" and the wicked one is a liar, then the whole world has been lied to.

Why is this important? Because once I came to the realization that I had been lied to, the scales could be taken off of my eyes and I could begin to deal with my life in an honest, truthful manner.

I said this earlier in the introduction; if we could "fix" ourselves we would have done it by now. The problem is that we can't. But here is the good news. There is someone who can fix us. His name is Jesus.

But here is also where the rubber meets the road; we've got to acknowledge that we can't fix ourselves. Until we surrender our lives to Christ, our father is the devil, who is the father of lies. I was growing up to be a liar, just like my father the devil. This is not easy for most people to grasp, but the Bible teaches that until we've accepted God's grace of salvation by surrendering our lives to Jesus, we're sinners. That's just the simple truth. I had to humbly come to the realization that I had been lied to and in turn, I had lied to the people that were closest to me. I had lied to my family and friends, to myself and to God.

One of the lies people buy into is to blame everybody else for their problems in life. I finally came to the understanding that I couldn't blame my problems on anybody else. My choices that I made were the reason that I was in the situation that I was in. My parents weren't to blame. Neither were my brother and sisters, or my friends or my environment that I grew up in. I was raised to know right from wrong and when I began to make the wrong choices in life, they were my choices and I would be accountable for those choices.

In the last ten years of involvement in prison ministry, juvenile ministry, men's ministry and observing thousands of people that are going through major trials in life, one of the common things I've observed is that people want to blame their problems on other people or their circumstances. Now... I realize that some people have had very difficult circumstances; however, how someone chooses to react to those circumstances is the key. How is it that two people can come from the same environment and they will turn out completely different? The reason is because they chose to react in different ways. We all have choices to make in life and the fact is there are consequences for those choices.

Real healing starts at the place of accountability.

If we say that we have no sin, we deceive ourselves, and the truth is not in us. If we confess our sins, He is faithful and just to forgive us our sins and to cleanse us from all unrighteousness. If we say that we have not sinned, we make Him a liar, and His word is not in us. (1 John 1:8-10)

A major theme of the last days is the spirit of deception will increase. Jesus spoke about this, Paul warned of it and today that deception is rampant. Once I came to the place of owning my choices, confessing my sins and stopped lying to everybody, including myself, the healing process could begin.

We as a nation have also bought into a lie. We believe that our success came from our own talent. The strong work ethic that *used* to be part of the American way of life had a certain amount to do with our success; however, our true success as a nation came from the fact that we were formed as a Christian nation. God's hand of protection and blessing has been upon America; that... and the fact that we've always supported and stood with Israel are the real reasons for the success of our nation.

> *"Blessed is the nation whose God is the LORD" (Psalm 33:12).*

That word "LORD" when all the letters are capitalized, in the original Hebrew language is the word "Jehovah", which refers to the God of Abraham, Isaac, and Jacob, the God of Israel. In Genesis 12:3 the LORD said to Abraham, speaking about the nation of Israel...

> *"I will bless those who bless you,*
> *and I will curse those who curse you"*
> *(Genesis 12:3).*

Do not be deceived; we have been blessed because we have been known as a Christian nation and because of our support of Israel. As we have turned away from the LORD, we have begun to have problems that we don't seem to have the answers for. And if we continue to soften in our support for Israel, God's word is clear that we will suffer the consequences. As a matter of fact, we're already suffering the consequences.

When talking about the spirit of deception, both on a personal level and nationally, we have to ask ourselves a question. Where do we go for the truth, so we won't believe the lies? The answer is the Bible. Please take this from a man who has been successful, then lost everything and then had it all restored tenfold. The Bible is the real source for truth. I have taken these principles from the Bible and applied them to my life and they work.

The devil has gone so far as to put the belief in people's minds that the Bible is "no longer relevant". I hear people say, "It was written so long ago that it no longer applies in our world." These thoughts are lies from the enemy of your soul.

> *"The Word of God is alive and active, sharper than any two-edged sword, piercing even to the division of soul and spirit, and of the joints and marrow, and is a discerner of the thoughts and intents of the heart" (Hebrews 4:12).*

That means that we can read a verse that applies in our lives, then read that same verse a few years later and it can apply in a whole different way. It also says...

> *"Beloved, do not believe every spirit, but test the spirits, whether they are of God;*

because many false prophets have gone out into the world" (1 John 4:1).

The Bible should be our line of truth in the sand. We are not to believe everything we hear or read, but we should test those things to see if it they line up with the Word of God. If something goes contrary to His Word, then it's wrong. I will discuss this in greater length later.

Let me speak about another lie that is prevalent in our nation today. This would be the lie about our eternal destiny. I hear people say that they believe there is more than one way to get to heaven. That other faiths also lead to heaven. That we are all going to the same place in the end. It amazes me when I read that as many as 60% of confessing Christians believe there is more than one way to heaven. I also hear people say that they are basically good people, so they believe they'll go to heaven. Or that they were raised in church, so they're going to heaven. Or that they came from a great family, so they're going to heaven. Or that a loving God would never send anyone to hell. God doesn't send anyone to hell. If someone ends up in hell, they are the one who is responsible. God doesn't force us to accept Jesus. We have a choice. We can either choose to accept Christ or reject Christ. We make our own choice, but like I've said, that choice has consequences.

Jesus said, *"Whoever confesses Me before men, him I will also confess before My Father who is in heaven. But whoever denies Me before men, him I will also deny before My Father who is in heaven"* (Matthew 6:32, 33).

It is a personal choice that each one of us has to make. You can't choose Jesus for me and I can't choose Jesus for you.

One of the newest beliefs that is becoming popular is that hell doesn't really exist. I will shine the truth on this lie later, but for now... let's stay focused on the lie that there are many ways to get to heaven.

Please... I beg of you to listen to what I'm about to tell you. If there was any other way, *any other way* to get to heaven, then Jesus wouldn't have had to die the violent death that He died. Listen to Jesus's own words:

> *"I am the way, the truth, and the life. No one comes to the Father except through Me" (John 14:6).*

Now, I'm not the smartest person walking around...but I get this statement by Jesus! Think about it this way: if there was *any* other way to get to heaven, Jesus could have come down from the cross and said, "Listen... there's two other ways to get to heaven, go find them." But Jesus didn't say that, because there aren't two other ways, or four other ways. *Jesus is the only way to heaven!* Both in Matthew and in Luke it is recorded that Jesus even ask if there was another way...

> *"And Jesus withdrew from them about a stone's throw, and He knelt down and prayed, saying, 'Father, if it is Your will, take this cup away from Me; nevertheless not My will, but Yours, be done'" (Luke 22:41, 42).*

Jesus knew the beating He was about to endure, the pain He was about to suffer and the separation He would feel from His Father and so He asked if there was any other way out of this situation. And of course, we know what happened next. You see... there was no other way. Jesus *had* to be crucified, be put to death and be raised from the dead to fulfill the Scriptures and to provide the sacrifice for our sins that we can't provide. There was no other way... and there's still no other way. If you believe that there is *any* other way to get to heaven, then you have believed the worst kind of lie; a lie about your eternal destiny. Hell is a real place. Heaven is a real place. Jesus talked about both hell and heaven in real terms. Jesus is the *only* way to get to heaven. I am asking you to believe me that I'm telling you the truth. The ultimate lie will be if you end up in hell because you choose not to believe that Jesus is the only way.

> *"And we know that the Son of God has come and has given us an understanding, that we may know Him who is true; and we are in Him who is true, in His Son Jesus Christ. This is the true God and eternal life"* (1 John 5:20).

While we have *all* been lied to... once we've been born again; everything changes. Now we have the Spirit of Truth in us. We should begin to be able to discern between good and evil. There should be a new sensitivity to evil and towards good. This is what Jesus meant when He said...

> *"If you abide in My word, you are My disciples indeed. And you shall know the truth, and the truth shall set you free"* (John 8:31, 32).

Here the conclusion of the matter: there is a liar out there named Satan. He wants to destroy you and me. If we're to live a victorious life, we need to know the enemy is real and we need to arm ourselves with the truth to fight the battle. We've been lied to, but we *can* know the truth and win the battle!

Chapter 3

Time to Make a Choice

—ⱳ—

So... at this point, I'm in jail, locked up because of my horrible decisions. I've come to the realization that I can't talk my way out this time. My family loves me, but I've hurt them enough and been down this road for so long that they made the decision to leave me in jail. Remember, the judge has "no bonded" me, which means that I'm not getting out anyway.

There is a process that takes place in being locked up, which is not that much different from the process that happens with people who are going through something very difficult in life. The first thing that we do is try to get out. Please, someone get me out of this. The same thing happens to people as they enter a trial in life. Just get me out. Let this be over. And as I mentioned before, we naturally want to blame someone else for the trial.

But let me ask a question here...

What if this trial we are entering into is from the Lord? What if He wants to either correct us or do some type of work in us? Without a doubt I can tell you that the Lord's hand was involved in my incarceration. Without the Lord intervening, I could very well have been dead by now. How many times when we go through trials do we look back and see the Lord's handwriting on what happened to us? And it is always for our benefit. We needed correction. Or, He will use the trial to bring us into a deeper understanding of who He is. I've said this many times over the last ten years: God is more concerned about our eternal destiny than He is about our earthly comfort. I would like you to stop and think about that. Let me say it again: God is more concerned about our eternal destiny than He is about our earthly comfort. What if through the trial we are entering into, God wants to use that trial to break us and then we surrender our lives to Christ and we receive Salvation? Now that trial has been well worth the pain and suffering...

Speaking about Jesus,

> *...who, in the days of His flesh, when He had offered up prayers and supplications, with vehement cries and tears to Him who was able to save Him from death, and was heard because of His godly fear, though He was a Son, yet He learned obedience by the things which He suffered. And having been perfected, He became the Author of eternal Salvation to all who obey Him. (Hebrews 5:7-9)*

These are amazing verses. Jesus is always our greatest example. Jesus suffered and learned obedience through His suffering. And remember this, Jesus suffered innocently; He didn't suffer for doing anything wrong. I was in my trial because of my bad choices. And yet, if Jesus learned obedience through His suffering, not doing anything wrong, how much more should we be willing to learn obedience through our sufferings considering that none of us are perfect like Jesus was? Also in Hebrews...

My son, do not despise the chastening of the LORD, nor be discouraged when you are rebuked by Him: for whom the LORD loves He chastens, and scourges every son whom He receives. If you endure chastening, God will deal with you as sons; for what son is there whom a father does not chasten? But if you are without chastening, of which we all have become partakers, then you are illegitimate and not sons.

Furthermore, we have had human fathers who corrected us, and we paid them respect. Shall we not much more readily be in subjection to the Father of spirits and live? For they indeed for a few days chastened us as seemed best to them, but He for our profit, that we may be partakers of His holiness. Now, no chastening seems to be joyful for the present, but painful; nevertheless, afterward it yields the peaceful fruit of righteousness to those who have been trained by it. (Hebrews 12:5-11)

Notice that God always has a purpose for the "chastening" we go through. This may seem harsh, but as parents don't we correct our children? Why? Because first of all, they need correction and secondly, we know what's best for them. Well, doesn't God know what's best for us? Of course He does.

When I speak about going to prison, sometimes I make the statement, "My greatest thinking landed me in prison." Think about this: does any-body start out in life with the "goal" of eventually going to prison? Can you imagine asking a child "What do you want to be when you grow up?" and the child saying, "I want to be a convict"? It's absolutely ridiculous. No... my thoughts and decisions in life led me down the wrong road.

Now, let me make a point here. It's easy for the general public to say, "You broke the law... you deserve what you got." I get that, I really do. But, let me ask a question. How many of you reading this book right now can honestly say, "I have never broken the law?" Never had two beers or two glasses of wine and drove home? Never smoked pot? Ever take something from work that wasn't yours? You've *never* broke the law? Then we need *you* in Washington! Here's my point... there *are* some people that are locked up and that's exactly where they need to be. However, most of the people behind bars are not that different from you, but they got caught. Many people in jail made bad choices, got caught and are now paying the price for their choices. The last unit that I was at there were 2,200 inmates and 1,400 were there for DWI. In Texas, if you get two DWIs in a certain amount of time, the judge can sentence you to prison. Now, I am not making any excuses. And I believe I got what I deserved. But we have to be careful in judging others. Thank God that He doesn't give me what I really deserve. We *all* would spend eternity in hell if we got what we really deserved. We all have a problem that we share and that problem is *sin*. We may not like that statement, but the Bible teaches that we're born with a sin nature.

Listen to these verses...

> *David said..."I was brought forth in iniquity, and in sin my mother conceived me"* (Psalm 51:5). And this was King David... who God said... "I have found David the son of Jesse, a man after My own heart, who will do all My will" (Acts 13:22).

> *"There is none righteous, no, not one"* (Romans 3:10); "For all have sinned and fall short of the glory of God" (Romans 3:23).

> *"There is a way that seems right to a man, but its end is the way of death"* (Proverbs 16:25).

Can I tell you something...? I need instruction in my life from a source that is smarter than I am... and so do you. And sometimes we *all* need correction. I know that I do.

So... here I was in jail and it was clear that I wasn't getting out. As I sat in my jail cell, day after day, I began to really consider my life up until that point. I can't speak for everyone, but many of us are simply "hard headed", for lack of a better way to describe it. How many times in life does a parent or someone else try to council us and we walk away thinking, "They don't get it," or, "They just don't understand"? Well guess what... perhaps it's *us* who don't "get it", who don't understand.

It became apparent to me that I was going to have to make a major change in my life. That may sound like a "duh" statement, but over the years since the Lord changed my life, I've observed that most people resist that major change until they hit "bottom". I've also observed that what may be the "bottom" for one person may not be the "bottom" for someone else. Well, for me, going to prison was hitting "bottom". And once I hit bottom I came to some harsh realizations about myself.

I will discuss some of these realizations in a later chapter, but for my purpose here, the point was that I needed to change. Once I came to that realization, the question became: what kind of change?

The first change that I needed to make was to stop the lies. As I mentioned before, one of the signs of the addict is the lies. We have lied to our family, our friends, ourselves and to the Lord. So it was time for me to stop lying.

I have to tell you that over the last ten years, as I made the decision to stop the lies and live my life with transparency, I've learned two things. One, that there is a tremendous peace and freedom that comes from living a life of transparency. What freedom there is when we don't have any secrets. Ask me something and I will tell you. There is great freedom and peace in that statement. The shame goes away. The condemnation goes away. The other thing I've learned is that most people don't have that transparency in their lives. You may disagree with that, but most people have areas that they don't want brought out into the light.

Everybody loves John 3:16. But read a few more verses and listen to what it says. Here are verses 16-21...

> *For God so loved the world that He gave His only begotten Son, that whoever believes in Him should not perish but have everlasting life. For God did not bring His Son into the world to condemn the world, but the world through Him might be saved. He who believes in Him is not condemned; but he who does not believe is condemned already, because he has not believed in the name of the only begotten Son of God.*
>
> *And this is the condemnation, that the light has come into the world, and men loved the darkness rather than the light, because their deeds were evil. For everyone practicing evil hates the light and does not come to the light, lest his deeds should be exposed. But he who does the truth comes to the light, that his deeds may be clearly seen, that they have been done in God.*

Many of us have those dark places; those secret places, those things that we hang onto because we're not ready for them to be brought out into the light. But those dark places are what I refer to as "blessing blockers". God may have something so awesome waiting for us, but He's waiting for us to come clean with Him. He already knows about these areas; He's God! But He's waiting on us to bring them out into the light. Only then can He take them away, cleanse us in the blood of Jesus and restore us. He loves us and is patiently waiting on us to come to Him. He wants us to be transparent with Him.

I mentioned in the introduction of this book that I have been granted a real peace that many others haven't been able to find. This transparency is a key to that peace. Let me give you two Scriptures that speak to this...

> *"Therefore, laying aside all malice, all deceit, hypocrisy, envy, and all evil speaking, as newborn babes, desire the pure milk of the word, that you may grow thereby, if indeed you have tasted that the Lord is gracious"* *(1 Peter 2:1-3).*

I have indeed tasted that the Lord is gracious. Many of us that the Lord has changed the most are the most grateful. That's why those who He has changed the most are also some of the boldest witnesses for Christ. We feel compelled to tell others about the goodness of God. Also...

> *"Looking carefully lest anyone fall short of the grace of God; lest any root of bitterness springing up cause trouble, and by this many become defiled"* *(Hebrews 12:15).*

I see so many people that are captured by bitterness, anger and envy. I mentioned before that I was in a physical prison, but these are all forms of bondage that keep people from the freedom and peace that I'm talking about.

I wanted real change in my life. So I knew that I had a choice to make.

I want to make mention of something here... these verses of Scripture that I mention have been part of the process over several years that the Lord has used to transform my life. It didn't happen overnight... and I have spent many, many hours meditating on God's word. There is a peace that comes from His word. But real change takes time. That's what James is talking about when he says...

"But let patience have its perfect work, that you may be mature and complete, lacking nothing" (James 1:4).

So I had to make a choice... and the choice that I made involved a real decision on my part. I made the decision, a conscious choice, to believe that the Bible was true; that it was the living Word of God. I knew that this would be a radical choice. It would be a life changing choice. Sounds so simple... doesn't it? And you know what... it *is* simple! We make it so much harder than it really has to be.

In the book of Deuteronomy, the Lord told the people that if they would believe Him, trust Him and obey Him, they would be blessed and they would prosper and that He would take care of them...

Moses is speaking to the people of Israel, and he says...

For this commandment which I command you today is not too mysterious for you, nor is it too far off. It is not in heaven, that you should say, "Who will ascend into heaven for us and bring it to us, that we may hear it and do it?" Nor is it beyond the sea, that you should say, "Who will go over the sea for us and bring it to us, that we may hear it and do it?" But the word is very near you, in your mouth and in your heart that you may do it.

See, I have set before you today life and good, death and evil, in that I command you today to love the LORD your God, to walk in His ways, and to keep His commandments, His statutes, and His judgments, that you may live and multiply; and the LORD your God will bless you in the land which you go in to possess. But if your heart turns away so that you do not hear, and are drawn away, and worship other gods and serve them, I announce to you today that you shall surely perish; you shall not prolong your days in the land which you cross over the Jordan to go in to possess.

I call heaven and earth as witnesses today against you, that I have set before you life and death, blessing and cursing; therefore choose life, that both you and your descendants may live; that you may love the LORD your God, that you may obey His voice, and that you may cling to Him, for He is your life and the length of your days; and that you may dwell in the land which the LORD swore to your fathers, to Abraham, Isaac, and Jacob, to give them. (Deuteronomy 30:11-20)

Please take note that we have a *choice!* "Life and death; blessing and cursing; therefore choose life." Then I saw a verse in Joshua...

And if it seems evil to you to serve the LORD, choose for yourselves this day whom you will serve, whether the gods which your fathers served that we're on the other side of the River, or the gods of the Amorites, in whose land you dwell. But as for me and my house, we will serve the LORD. (Joshua 24:15)

When I read these verses for the first time, I said to myself, "That's it... I'm done! I'm making the choice from this point forward to believe this Bible... to commit my life to Jesus Christ. I may not always understand; I'm sure I'll stumble. I will probably be laughed at, ridiculed, scoffed at and made fun of, but I don't care. I am going to, to the best of my ability, follow Christ. And there will be no turning back."

I remember... I was in my cell and I stood up, drew an imaginary line across the floor and I stepped over it. I said "That's it... I surrender." The next thing I did was hit my knees and gave my life to Jesus Christ. I had made my choice! I chose to surrender my life to Jesus as my Lord and my Savior.

"LORD, I thank You that You didn't give up on me when You could have; when You probably should have. I thank You that You loved me enough to chasten me when I needed it the most. Even now

I can still see Your handwriting on my life. What an awesome God You are, that You are mindful of someone like me. And yet LORD, there are others out there who are wandering... who are lost in their travels through life that need a touch from You... the Master. You give us choices Father... and many, many times we choose the wrong path. So now I ask in the name of Your Son Jesus Christ that in Your sovereignty You will help those who need You to choose life. That they will choose Jesus... and come to know true peace in this chaotic world. Thank You Father that You loved us enough to make a way through Your Son for us to come home. In Jesus's Name I pray... Amen."

Chapter 4

I Surrender

—ɯ—

Ok... I surrender! But what exactly does that mean? If I was going to really surrender my life to Jesus Christ, what would that look like? It was Gandhi who said, "I admire Christ, but not Christians." Most of us can certainly relate to that. Even to this day when people say, "You are very religious," it makes me cringe. While I wasn't sure what my life would look like as a Christian, I was sure what I didn't want it to look like.

I always thought most "religions" were hypocritical. I still do. I also thought Christians we're supposed to be different... the problem was that most people I knew or had seen that claimed to be Christians really didn't act much different than everybody else... they went to the same bars... did the same things... used the same language... so to me that seemed hypocritical as well. So I began to look through the Bible to see if it said anything about Christians living differently and I was surprised that the Bible had a great deal to say about the subject.

"'Come out from among them and be separate,' says the Lord. 'Do not touch

what is unclean, and I will receive you. I will be a Father to you, and you shall be My sons and daughters,' says the Lord Almighty" (2 Corinthians 6:17).

I had spent enough of my life touching what was unclean, so this sounded like a call to a different kind of life all together. Just because you go to church for an hour on Sunday, that doesn't make you a Christian. That's *not* what I wanted. I knew that my life had to change in a drastic way. I also knew that I wanted a real, tangible faith that would involve a complete surrender on my part.

We've all met a few people in our lives that we look at and think, "That's a Godly person." It might be a grandmother, a teacher, or a parent. One thing is for sure; there is something different about that person. We look at that person and think, "I want what they have." There is a peace, a presence, a sense of wisdom about them. They're not religious. They're not hypocritical. Their walk matches their talk. They're real, authentic and they take their faith seriously. You just know that Jesus Christ is the center of their lives. And when the storms in life come (and they will come) they're on solid ground. That's what I wanted.

I didn't want to play with God. No more deceit. I wanted to be able to be real with God; to be able to pour out my heart to Him, to tell Him anything with no secrets, to talk with Him when I'm angry, sad, happy, confused or frustrated. I want to be able to pray to Him about everything and anything. I want to know Him, to understand Him, to trust Him, to believe Him. I want a real relationship with Him, the Creator of the universe and I want Him to be my Father.

And I knew *this*: I needed a Savior! I couldn't save myself. And not only did I need a Savior, I needed that Savior to change my life. My life was a train wreck and I needed a complete overhaul. Does that sound familiar to anyone else out there? I needed *a lot* of forgiveness. I had hurt a lot of people. I needed to get to the place where I could forgive myself for all the pain I had caused others. And of course I needed forgiveness from the LORD. I would need Jesus to change my morals, values, attitudes, habits, my decision making process, even my language.

I looked up the word "surrender" in the dictionary. It means "to yield to the power, control, or possession of another; to give up completely; to give oneself up into the power of another". That's exactly what I needed to do.

Let me show you a great example of that in the Bible. In Isaiah 6 we read about the calling of Isaiah. Here's the setting: King Uzziah had just died. Tradition has it that Isaiah was King Uzziah's nephew. Imagine that the King has just died and he's your uncle. Isaiah's world was rocked. He was devastated. Just like most of us today, often times a tragedy is what it takes to really get our attention. Obviously, that's what it took with me.

> *In the year that King Uzziah died, I saw the Lord sitting on a throne, high and lifted up, and the train of His robe filled the temple. Above it stood seraphim, each one had six wings: with two he covered his face, with two he covered his feet, and with two he flew. And one cried to*

another and said: "Holy, holy, holy is the LORD of hosts; the whole earth is full of His glory!" and the posts of the door were shaken by the voice of him who cried out, and the house was filled with smoke.

So I said: "Woe is me, for I am undone! Because I am a man of unclean lips, and I dwell in the midst of a people of unclean lips; for my eyes have seen the King, the LORD of hosts." Then one of the seraphim flew to me, having in his hand a live coal which he had taken with the tongs from the altar, and he touched my mouth with it, and said: "Behold, this has touched your lips; your iniquity is taken away, and your sin purged." Also I heard the voice of the Lord saying: "Whom shall I send, and who will go for Us?" Then I said, "Here am I! Send me." (Isaiah 6:1-9)

I have spent many hours studying and meditating on these verses over the last ten years. Allow me to share some thoughts. First of all, it jumps out to me who is writing this. This isn't some average guy writing this. Referred to as *the* prophet, this is Isaiah. The book of Isaiah stands at the peak of the Old Testament. Isaiah is quoted over and over again in the New Testament. His book has more chapters than any other prophetic book and looks farther into the future than any other Old Testament book. Just his name, which means "Yahweh is Salvation", says so much. And yet this man said, "Woe is me, for I am undone! Because I am a man of unclean lips, and I dwell in the midst of a people with unclean lips." The word "woe" was a legal term meaning "ruined or dead". He then says, "I am undone", which is a declaration of total self-condemnation. In essence he was saying "I am dead... I am speechless!" He then pronounces that he's "unclean", which meant "defiled". Why did Isaiah declare these things? Because, he said, "my eyes have seen the King, the LORD of hosts."

Isaiah got a realistic vision of who God really is. The God of Holiness; the God of Righteousness; the God of Purity; the Almighty Jehovah God! And when Isaiah got a real vision of who God is, he was done! I have stopped, gotten still and meditated about this for hours at a time. We would *all* do well to stop and meditate about who God really is. Our minds can't comprehend who He really is, but we should try. When I think about God like this, I find myself speechless as well. He alone is worthy to be praised.

In my opinion, this is the starting place in surrendering our lives to Jesus Christ. Until we understand that God is a Holy God and until we have a proper perspective on our sin, we can't appreciate the gift that He has given us in His Son Jesus. The fact that He loved someone like me enough to send His only Son to die for me; I don't have the words to express my gratitude. I'm speechless. I certainly don't deserve salvation. I deserve hell. We all deserve hell. But He is the God of Grace, the God of Mercy, the God of Forgiveness, the God of Love. Let that sink in for a few moments... the Bible says He knows us by name.

> *"But now," thus says the LORD, who*
> *created you, O Jacob, and He who*

formed you, O Israel: "Fear not, for I have redeemed you; I have called you by your name; you are Mine. When you pass through the waters, I will be with you; and through the rivers, they shall not overflow you. When you walk through the fire, you shall not be burned. Nor shall the flame scorch you, for I am the LORD your God, the Holy One of Israel, your Savior." (Isaiah 43:1-3)

I personalize the Scriptures; you should too.

"For You formed my inward parts; You covered me in my mother's womb. I will praise You, for I am fearfully and wonderfully made; marvelous are Your works and that my soul knows very well" (Psalm 139:13, 14).

The LORD made us. And when we get a proper perspective on who He is; similar to Isaiah did, it should cause us to say as well, "Woe is me; for I am undone."

Notice the first thing that happened after Isaiah got a vision of the LORD...

Then one of the seraphim flew to me, having in his hand a live coal which he had taken with the tongs from the altar, and he touched my mouth with it and said: "Behold, this has touched your lips; Your iniquity is taken away, and your sin purged." (Isaiah 6:6, 7)

After seeing the LORD, Isaiah's lips were touched and his sin was taken away. The LORD changed Isaiah's speech. That's the first thing the LORD did with me. I used to swear all the time. I had a horrible language problem, but the LORD changed that. At the point of surrender; the LORD begins the process of changing us...

Verse 8 says, *"Also I heard the voice of the Lord, saying 'Whom shall I send, and who will go for Us.' Then I said, 'Here am I! Send me.'"*

After the vision of seeing the LORD, now Isaiah can hear the Lord. He became sensitive to the things of God. Again, at the point of surrender, we can now begin to understand God's word in a way we couldn't before. We are able to hear the word of the Lord. I have met many people over the years who say this: "Before I got saved, I couldn't understand the Bible, but after I got saved, it made sense to me." That happened to me as well.

Jesus said over and over again, *"He who has ears to hear, let him hear!" (Mark 4:9).*

Finally, after seeing the LORD and the Lord saying, "Who will go for Us?" Isaiah says, "Here am I! Send me." Isaiah wants to "witness" what he has seen, and what he has heard. That's also what happens after we surrender our lives to Jesus. We want to tell someone. The Lord has changed me. I have to tell other people about what He has done in my life. We're called to be witnesses. Jesus said, "You shall be witnesses to Me."

Allow me to pour out my heart here. Part of surrendering to Jesus Christ for me was coming to my right mind. It was very humbling to think that I had wasted so many years of my life. All the years of living a life of no value. When I thought of the abilities that the LORD had blessed me with, instead of using those talents for the Kingdom of God, I had squandered them. There was guilt and shame that I had been duped into thinking that I had ever had the right to live my life independent of God. This was the first time that I had ever really stopped to think that my life was not my own. That my body was His to do what He wanted with. I remember coming across this verse...

> *"When I was a child, I spoke as a child, I understood as a child, I thought as a child; but when I became a man, I put away childish things" (1 Corinthians 13:11).*

Coming to the realization that I had lived a life of selfishness... that there was more to life than Craig Nedrow. That there were other people that were affected by my stupid choices in life and that I needed to grow up.

I'm done, LORD. My life as I know it is over with. You take my life from here on out and do what You want with it.

So... at this point; I've surrendered my life to Christ. I know that I will never be the same. I don't yet know what I will be, but I know that things from here on out are going to be different. This is the start of a new journey in my life. The "old" Craig has just died... now begins life as the "new" Craig.

What's next, LORD?

Chapter 5

The Word of God

—⚊—

Once we've surrendered our lives to Jesus Christ, everything will change.

> *"Therefore, if anyone is in Christ, they are a new creation; old things have passed away; behold, all things have become new" (2 Corinthians 5:17).*

Notice there it says *"all"* things have become new." It doesn't say "some things have become new; or most things have become new." No, it says "ALL".

Our old habits... thoughts... values... viewpoints... language... even many of our relationships will have to become new.

In prison they teach that the definition for "insanity" is doing the same thing over and over again and expecting different results. I tell men in prison... "if you go back to the same neighborhood and hang out with the same people and do the same things, you can expect the same results." The same principal applies with our new life in Christ. I'm talking about a "radical" life change.

The reason this chapter is titled "The Word of God" is because that's primarily how the Lord speaks to us – through His word. I can tell you without any hesitation that God changed my life through His word. When I mentioned earlier that the word of God is "alive and active", that's such an amazing statement. It means that we can personalize God's word. It means that God's word applied when it was written and it still applies today. We shouldn't think that God's word applied back then, but that it no longer applies today. That's a lie from the enemy and many people have fallen for that lie.

If we will get to the place where we can believe God's word and stop doubting His word, there is no end to what He can do. Listen to what God says about His word...

> *"So shall My word be that goes forth from My mouth; it shall not return to Me void, but it shall accomplish what I please, and it shall prosper in the thing for which I sent it" (Isaiah 55:11).*

God is saying here that His word, that would be the Bible, will yield results. It says that His word will "prosper"; that means it will "be profitable in". It says in the "thing which I sent it"; that means if we will receive the word of God, then we're the "thing" in which He sent it. Our part is to receive the word of God and believe the word of God...

> *"If you will not believe, surely you shall not be established" (Isaiah 7:9).*

I now base my entire life on God's word, the Bible. I believe God's word. I pray God's word; I stand on God's word; I trust God's word. And please hear me... God's word will do what He says it will do. He has changed everything in my life. But first I had to settle it in my own mind that I would believe and trust His word. If this sounds simple... that's because it *is* simple. We make it so much harder than it has to be.

> Jesus said, *"You are already clean because of the word which I have spoken to you"* (John 15:7).

The word of God has a cleansing effect on us that can't be explained in the natural. I needed that cleansing. I needed my mind cleansed of all the garbage that had been there for so long. I needed my heart cleansed from the selfishness that was part of me. The arrogance, the self-pride, the rebellious spirit that is in all of us has to be cleansed away by the blood of Christ and the washing of His word.

> *"Your words were found, and I ate them, and Your word was to me the joy and rejoicing of my heart; for I am called by Your name, O LORD God of hosts"* (Jeremiah 15:16).

In my Bible when I found this verse I wrote, "I love this passage" in the margin. When I was locked away, I began to spend ten to twelve hours a day studying the word of God. I began to find promises in His word that I could base the rest of my life on. Let me share just a few of these life changing Scriptures with you.

(1) Jesus said, *"The Helper, the Holy Spirit, whom the Father will send in My name, He will teach you all things, and bring to your remembrance all things that I said to you"* (John 14:26).

I like Study Bibles, concordances and the such, but my teacher is the Holy Spirit. Jesus said He would send the Holy Spirit who would teach us all things. So, to this day, when I sit down to read and study the Bible, I stop and ask the Holy Spirit to teach me, to open my mind, to give me understanding of what He wants me to know. That's how I approach the Scriptures. We begin by reading the word. Then we go a little deeper and we study the word. That means we may look at the setting in which a particular passage was written; we take into consideration who wrote the passage; who the passage was written to. What were the circumstances surrounding the passage? We may look at key words in the passage in the original language because we lose much of the meaning in translating a Hebrew or Greek or Aramaic word into the English language. All these things help us to have a deeper understanding of the Scripture. Then we go even deeper and begin meditating on the word. That means we take a verse or passage and read it over and over and over. We stop and think about the passage; we ask the Holy Spirit to show us what God wants to teach us from that passage. We go back and read it again and again. What happens when we do this? That passage begins to manifest itself. The Holy Spirit begins to minister to us about how that passage applies to us. How that passage can change us; how it can transform us...

> (2) *"And do not be conformed to this world, but be transformed by the renewing of your mind" (Romans 12:2).*

Our minds are renewed through prayer and through the word of God. That's what was happening to me as I spent hours and hours in His word. There are two words in this verse to take note of. The word "conformed" there in the original Greek means "to be molded" or "made the same as". So, we're told not to be "made the same as" the world, not to "be molded to" the world. The problem is that most of us *have* been molded to the world, but here God's word tells us *not* to be molded to the world. That brings us to the second key word in the passage: "transformed". That word in the Greek is the word *metamorphoo,* where we get the word "metamorphosis", which means "an abrupt developmental change", "a striking alteration in appearance, character, and/or circumstances". So... not only are we told that we're *not* "to be molded" to the world, but we're also told that we are to be "strikingly altered in appearance, character, and/or circumstances." To me... this is an amazing statement! And this is done by the renewing of our mind. This calls for a complete "overhaul" of the mind. Now do you understand why I say that this is a "radical" change? There is no way else to describe it...

> (3) *"Be still and know that I am God"* (Psalm 46:10).

That sounds like such a simple verse, but let me give you a glimpse into what this verse has meant to me. Remember that I talked about meditating on a passage... I have spent thousands of hours on this verse. My wife found this verse on a plaque that hangs in our home. Let me break it down.

Will you do something here please... read these next few paragraphs very slowly... maybe even read them several times and let them sink in.

First of all... it says, "Be still." Are you kidding me? "Be still"? In the world we live in today? Just these two words go against everything that our world is about. Our world says... "Hurry up... Get more done... Manage your time... Time is money... Just do it... I gotta go..." But here God's word says, "Be still..."

The word "be" is a verb... it denotes action. Well didn't you just say that we're to "be still"? When I say it denotes action, I mean we have to be deliberate about it. That means we have to be deliberate about getting "still". It means we have to purposely get "still". The word "still" is the Hebrew word *raphah*, which means, "to cease", "to faint", "to become idle", "to hang limp". In our world... it means that we're to "shut down"... "to get quiet"... "to clear our minds." To me... there is a peace to this word. It means turn your cell phone *off*... find a place that you consider peaceful, whether that's a comfortable chair at home, or by a creek somewhere, or on your back porch and get alone. That's right, alone. Then... just stop what you're doing... pause... get quiet... breathe... close your eyes for a minute or two... just relax... that's it..."be still"... "and know".

The word "know" in the Hebrew is a very "special" word. This word has a deep meaning in the Hebrew language. It's the word *yada*. It means "careful consideration, close observation, recognition in a close and personal way, intimate relationship, kinfolk, intimacy". Do you see what I mean when I say this is a "special" word? This doesn't mean to just know something on the surface... it means to know in the most personal, intimate, deep way. Think about something: to really know someone this deeply, don't you have to spend time with them? You have to spend time listening to them, talking to them, getting to know their personality, what they like and don't like, what their opinions are, where they stand on things. If it sounds like a love relationship – that's because what I'm describing *is* a love relationship! That's what this word *yada* means. "Be still... and know... that I am God." He is God... let me say that again... first with the emphasis on *"He"*... Who is God? *He* is God! I'm not God... you're not God... *He* is God. Notice that... *He*...not me, not we ...but *He!* We need to understand that *He* is God; not us and that *He* doesn't need any help from us to *be* God. It's who *He is!* Now... allow me to show you that verse again...

> *"Be still, and know that I am God"*
> *(Psalm 46:10).*

Now think about this... When we're in church, praising and worshiping Him, or listening to a sermon, or attending a Bible study, we know that "He is God"... But how about when we find out that we lost our job... or that a spouse has cheated on us... or that a loved one has died unexpectedly... or that a partner in business has stolen from us... do we know that "He is God" then? When Job lost his entire family and all his possessions, he said...

> *"Shall we indeed accept good from God, and shall we not accept adversity?"* *(Job 2:10).*

...He is God in the good times and the trouble times. He is on His throne now... He's always been on His throne... and He always will be on His throne. Nothing we do shocks God... nothing ever happens that has God wringing His hands saying, "Wow, I didn't see *that* coming!"

> *"I am the LORD, I do not change"* *(Malachi 3:6).*

> *"Jesus Christ is the same yesterday, today, and forever" (Hebrews 13:8).*

We change, He doesn't; we falter, He doesn't; we stumble, He doesn't; we're unfaithful, He's faithful. Glory be to Himself that He is who He is!

> *"I am the Alpha and the Omega; the Beginning and the End," says the Lord, "who is and who was and who is to come, the Almighty" (Revelation 1:8).*

...And He's our Father in heaven; He's our Lord and Savior Jesus Christ; He's the Holy Spirit who dwells within us. *Hallelujah!*

Are you beginning to understand what I mean about meditating on a verse? This small verse is one of my very favorite passages in all of Scripture.

The Bible is not just a book. It is a living, breathing covenant.

> *"Knowing this first, that no prophecy of Scripture is of any private interpretation, for prophecy never came by the will of man, but holy men of God spoke as they were moved by the Holy Spirit"* (2 Peter 1:20, 21).

Over the centuries, people have tried to destroy the Bible; they have tried to outlaw the Bible; they have tried to trivialize the Bible, all unsuccessfully. Every year the Bible outsells all other books many times over. It is translated in more languages than any other book many times over. People have and will continue to die for the Bible. This is God's word and it is alive.

How we approach the Bible is crucial for us both individually and as a nation. Let me explain what I mean.

In the world today I come across so many people who don't believe the Bible is the word of God. This is tragic. Stop and think about something. Go with me here... let's just assume that the Bible is exactly what it says it is: the living word of God. If that's true, then how arrogant is it to make comments like: "I don't think the Bible applies in today's world" or "I have a problem with the Bible in this area or that area" or "the Bible is no longer relevant" or "It's hate speech". A person should be very careful about the comments he or she makes about God's word. What if you're wrong? Can you imagine standing before God Almighty after making those kinds of statements about His word? What has happened to the "fear of the Lord" in our nation today?

> *"The fear of the Lord is the beginning of knowledge. But fools despise wisdom and instruction" (Proverbs 1:7, 9:10).*

That means that the lack of knowledge and wisdom would be the lack of the "fear of the Lord".

The Bible says in the last days there will be "scoffers" and "mockers" and those who will treat God and His word with contempt and we are certainly there today.

> *Knowing this first; that scoffers will come in the last days, walking according to their own lusts, and saying, "Where is the promise of His coming? For since the fathers fell asleep, all things continue as they were from the beginning of creation." (2 Peter 3:3, 4)*

Now... listen to me: I am not speaking from a position of arrogance. I am not trying to offend anyone, but I am speaking from a sincere heart. Take it from someone who lived for years on the run from God. I knew that He existed... but I wasn't ready to hear about Him or His word. I was arrogant... I was rebellious... I was blind... But now I see. I have no ulterior motive when I speak about these things other than a desire for people to experience the freedom and peace that the Lord has granted to me. That and as a nation, if we would just humble ourselves and return to the authority of the word of God, then He would heal our land.

When I shut up heaven and there is no rain, or command the locusts to devour the land, or send pestilence among My people, if My people who are called by My name will humble themselves, and pray and seek My face, and turn from their wicked ways, then I will hear from heaven, and will forgive their sin and heal their land. (2 Chronicles 7:13, 14)

Notice two things here: (1) He will heal our land! We won't, we can't; only He can. (2) Sometimes it *is* God who will "shut up heaven", "command the locusts to devour the land", or "send pestilence among His people". Why would God do these things? Because the people have rebelled against His word. Over and over again God reminds His people that obedience to His word brings blessings and disobedience brings correction. Listen to His warning...

"Return, backsliding Israel," says the LORD; "I will not cause My anger to fall on you. For I am merciful," says the LORD; "I will not remain angry forever. Only acknowledge your iniquity, that you have transgressed against the LORD your God, and have scattered your charms to alien deities under every green tree, and have not obeyed My voice," says the LORD. "Return, O backsliding children, says the LORD; for I am married to you." (Jeremiah 3:12-14)

Can't you feel the heartbeat of our Father? He says..."just acknowledge your iniquity," as a loving parent He says... "You know what you've done and I know what you've done... just confess it and return to Me." Why have we in America turned from God's word? It's a spirit of arrogance... a spirit of rebellion. God's word is still the same pure word it always has been...

> *"The words of the LORD are pure words, like silver tried in a furnace of earth, purified seven times" (Psalm 12:6).*

It's interesting that it says..."purified seven times." In the Bible, the number seven always represents perfection. God's word is perfect... God's word is pure... God's word is truth! And God's word is the final authority...

> *"All flesh is as grass, and all the glory of man as the flower of the grass. The grass withers, and its flower falls away, but the word of the LORD endures forever. Now this is the word which by the gospel was preached to you" (1 Peter 1:24, 25).*

Please listen to me: the word of the LORD changed my life. I can't overemphasize the magnitude of that. And when I say "changed", I mean in a radical way.

Something that grieves me greatly... I see many people that are really suffering... and they are searching for answers to their suffering. I have talked to many people who have been in recovery program after recovery program. I listen to all these twelve step programs refer to a "Higher Power". Listen to me...

The "Higher Power" has a name: His name is *Jesus Christ!* The devil loves it when we call it a "Higher Power" as we know it. That's like putting a Band-Aid on a gunshot wound. Until we stop the madness... people will still suffer. These recovery programs put the focus on "me, me, me..." Get the focus off of "me" and get the focus on Jesus Christ. Only Jesus can really and truly heal us. I've gone with friends to AA or NA and I hear someone say, "My name's Bob or Jim, and I'm a drug addict, and I've been clean for such and such amount of time and it's still a day to day struggle..." Well..."My name is Craig, I am a child of the Lord Jesus Christ, and I have been redeemed, filled with the Holy Spirit, sanctified and it's *not* a day to day struggle! I don't have cravings... I don't think about relapsing... because I've been delivered from my addiction." I want to scream from the highest mountain that I've found the answer! It's *Jesus!* Stop looking everywhere else..."Come to Jesus..."

> *"Come to Me, all you who labor and are heavy laden, and I will give you rest. Take My yoke upon you and learn from Me, for I am gentle and lowly in heart, and you will find rest for your souls, for My yoke is easy and My burden is light"* *(Matthew 11:28-30).*

If you're suffering, let me ask you a question... aren't you *tired?* You're not meant to carry this... Jesus said "Come to Me... just come to Me..." He's still saying that now... His name is Jesus... just come to Him...

I invite you to come to Jesus...

Chapter 6

The Wilderness

—ɷ—

As we look at the topic of being in the wilderness, allow me to point out something. Just so you'll know, when we're in the wilderness we're in great company. Here's a small list of characters who had their own wilderness experiences: Abraham... Moses... David... Ezekiel... Paul... and of course, always our greatest example... Jesus. We will take a closer look at some of these examples, but first let's talk about the concept of "The Wilderness" experience.

We can enter into the wilderness in different ways: it may be that everything seems to going along just fine in life and then over a period of time things begin to veer off track. It can be very subtle at first and then we begin to realize that things are starting to happen that are disrupting our flow in life. We all have our "comfort zone" and we begin to feel ourselves being pulled out of that zone. Our boat begins to rock. We're not sure what's happening, but something's going on. Sound familiar to anyone? Within a matter of time we find ourselves in a storm of life. One day soon we stop and realize we're in a lonely place, where our world as we knew it has suddenly taken a turn in a totally different direction. Welcome to the wilderness.

Another way that we enter into the wilderness is very suddenly. It can be a drastic event that we have caused ourselves or it can be some traumatic situation that we're suddenly thrown into that's not any fault of our own. Either way we end up there; this is what I refer to as a wilderness experience.

When we enter into the wilderness, it's our nature to react in some way. Often times the first reaction is to try and get out of what we're entering into. Because we've been taken out of that "comfort zone", we just want to get back there. We begin to look for others to blame for what's happening. We may even be quick to blame ourselves. Yet, the Bible has something to say about these wilderness times...

> *"My brethren, count it all joy when you fall into various trials, knowing that the testing of your faith produces patience. But let patience have its perfect work, that you may be mature and complete, lacking nothing" (James 1:2-4).*

I remember when I first saw this verse. I was locked up and had just received a two year prison sentence. "Count it all joy" ...are you kidding me? This was a very difficult Scripture for me to read at the time. Allow me to give some counsel here: if you know someone who is in the early stages of a wilderness experience, use discernment before just quoting this verse to them. Spiritually speaking, they may not be in a place yet to receive this word.

Most of us think when we're in the wilderness that the devil is attacking us. While there are times that we may be under attack, let me ask a question here. What if, instead of the devil attacking us... the wilderness that we're in is actually the work of the Lord?

I can testify that it was not the devil that sent me to prison. The devil was perfectly content when I was running around out in the world, wasting my life.

I mentioned in an earlier chapter that the hand of the Lord was involved in me going to prison. What I had to face was that my life was out of control. God loved me enough that He had me arrested and no bonded, which meant that I wasn't getting out. I also mentioned in a previous chapter that I had a sister that prayed with her prayer group that I would be arrested and go to prison. That's very tough love. Now, in hindsight, that prayer was instrumental in saving my life.

What we should do in the wilderness experiences of life is... stop: ask the Lord this question... "What is it that You are doing in this experience? What do You want to do in me through this process?" Instead of trying to get ourselves out of the wilderness, imagine coming to the place of allowing the Holy Spirit to accomplish the work in us that He wants to. That's what this verse in James is talking about.

I mentioned a verse earlier that is one of my very favorite in the entire Bible...

"Be still and know that I am God"
(Psalm 46:10).

For me... it took going to prison to get still. I've said this before many times when I speak publicly; one of the greatest things that have ever happened to me was going to the penitentiary. That was the "tool" that the Lord used to get me still.

In Texas when a person goes to prison, they first go to what is called an "I.D. Unit". At the I.D. Unit it is determined where an inmate will do their time. For example, if someone has a two year sentence, they will not be housed at the same unit as an inmate serving a 20 year sentence. Or if someone is locked up for using drugs they will not be housed with someone that's in for aggravated assault with a deadly weapon.

At the I.D. Unit that I went to, I was told that I had been chosen for an experimental program that the Texas Department of Corrections (TDC) was starting. I was told later that this was the first Faith Based Program in the State of Texas. There were 173 men that had been chosen for this program. I was sent to a small unit in East Texas. I was in lock down 22 hours a day.

We had Bible study seven days a week; church seven nights a week. This is when I began spending ten to twelve hours a day in the word of God. At 10 P.M. It was lights out. The only reason an inmate could be off his bunk was if he was at the day tables either writing a letter or studying the Bible. This was the only time it would get quiet, so I began studying at ten and without even realizing it I would still be up studying when the guards brought breakfast in at six in the morning. That's eight hours. Then after breakfast I would go to sleep until about noon when lunch would come in. Then after lunch I would study from about one until afternoon Bible study at three o'clock.

In an average week, there would be four to six different pastors from East Texas that would teach

Bible study. In some strange way, for lack of a better way to describe it, this felt like living in a monastery. Out of the 173 inmates in this program, there were only a handful of us that were spending that significant amount of time in the word of God. It was during this period that I came to love the word of God so deeply.

> *"Your words were found, and I ate them. And Your word was to me the joy and rejoicing of my heart, for I am called by Your name, O LORD God of hosts"* (Jeremiah 15:16).

We don't hear much preaching from the book of Jeremiah, which is sad because it's an amazing book about a man that grieved as he witnessed his nation turn from the Lord. Over and over the Lord called the nation back, warning the people that if they would just confess, repent and return to Him all would be well, but if they didn't they would be destroyed as a nation. For 23 years the Lord used Jeremiah to warn the nation and yet they refused to heed those warnings. And because of their rebellious actions, the nation was destroyed and taken captive by King Nebuchadnezzar. The book of Jeremiah should be a lesson for our nation today that there are conse-quences for a nation that turns away from the Lord. I spent almost four months in the book of Jeremiah. This was an amazing time in my life.

One of the pastors that were teaching Bible studies said to me, "This is your wilderness experience." The wilderness is where the deep spiritual work is done in our lives. Think about something: during the good times most of us don't really seek the Lord; it's when something traumatic happens that we cry out to Him. That's our human nature. That's why sometimes it's the Lord who takes us out into the wilderness – so He can break us, refine us and transform us. I'm a witness to the process.

I mentioned some of the people that had wilderness experiences. Let's take a quick look at a few.

First of all, let's look at Abraham...

> *"Now the LORD had said to Abram: 'Get out of your country, from your family. And from your father's house, to a land that I will show you'" (Genesis 12:1).*

Notice that the LORD is the one who called Abram out into the wilderness. God told him to leave his country, his family and in particular his father's house. Does this sound drastic to you? Often times God calls us to drastic measures. He will take us into a wilderness where we come to an understanding that we have no one else but Him. We will be taken to a place away from all our familiar surroundings, including our loved ones. Why would God do this? Because we have to get to that place of brokenness where we are totally reliant upon Him and Him alone. For me, I had to lose everything and come to the end of myself. I came to the realization that my only hope was Him. It's at that place that we cry out to Him and seek Him with all of our heart. This is crucial to remember: God *always* has our best interest in mind. He knows what's best for us and has a plan for us...

> *"For I know the thoughts that I think toward you," says the LORD, "thoughts of peace and not of evil, to give you a*

*future and a hope. Then you will call
upon Me and go and pray to Me, and I will
listen to you. And you will seek Me and
find Me, when you search for Me with all
your heart. I will be found by you, says
the LORD, and I will bring you back from
your captivity." (Jeremiah 29:11-14)*

Please notice that it says there... "And you will
seek Me and find Me, when you search for Me with
all your heart." That's exactly what happened with
me. I found the LORD when I searched for Him with
all my heart. If we will allow Him to have His way
with us in the wilderness, He will change us in ways
that we can't imagine. To Abram, God said...

*"I will make you a great nation; I will
bless you and make your name great;
and you shall be a blessing. I will bless
those who bless you, and I will curse
him who curses you; and in you all the
families of the earth shall be blessed"
(Genesis 12:2, 3).*

God went on to say...

*No longer shall your name be called
Abram, but your name shall be Abraham;
for I have made you a father of many
nations. I will make you exceedingly
fruitful; and I will make nations of you,
and kings shall come from you. And I
will establish My covenant between Me
and you and your descendants after you
in their generations, for an everlasting*

covenant, to be God to you and your descendants after you. (Genesis 17:5-7)

Let me make a few points here...

First: The LORD changed Abram's name to Abraham. Much more than in our world today... names at that time were very important. The name Abraham means "father of many nations". In other words, God gave Abram a whole new identity. Now, every time someone called Abram by his name, they were saying, "you're Abraham, father of many nations". When we allow God to have His way with us in the wilderness experiences, He will completely change our identity. The LORD did that with me. Glory to God!

Second: When the LORD told Abram to leave his family and his country and took him out into the wilderness, Abram could have doubted God, but he didn't.

> *"For what does the Scripture say?" Abraham believed God, and it was accounted to him for righteousness" (Romans 4:3).*

It's easy to believe God when everything is going great... but what about when things aren't going so well? How about when He takes us out into the wilderness? When we're confused about what's going on in our life? Will we trust Him then?

> *"Trust in the LORD with all your heart, and lean not on your own understanding; in all your ways acknowledge Him, and He will direct your paths" (Proverbs 3:5, 6).*

As hard as this may be, we need to stop trying to figure everything out and learn to trust God. I'm not stupid, but my greatest thinking landed me in prison. We're not as smart as we think we are. Can you imagine really trusting the LORD and allowing Him to lead our lives? He has the answers to our personal problems as well as our nation's problems. When we began to turn from God as a nation, that's when we started having problems that we can't figure out. God has the answers when we don't...

> *"For My thoughts are not your thoughts, nor are your ways My ways," says the LORD. For as the heavens are higher than the earth, so are My ways higher than your ways, and My thoughts than your thoughts" (Isaiah 55:8, 9).*

What an awesome thought... that we can trust the Creator of the universe to direct our paths, to give us the wisdom we need to live our lives. Yes, Abraham believed God... and we can still believe God.

Finally, when we trust God in the wilderness experiences of life like Abraham did, He will bless us in ways that we can't imagine. He made Abraham the Father of many nations... and even greater than that...

> *"This book of the genealogy of Jesus Christ, the Son of David, the Son of Abraham" (Matthew 1:1).*

God put Abraham in the family lineage of Jesus Christ! Allow me to testify personally about something... While still in prison, I began to journal. In this journal I poured out my deepest fears, dreams and hopes. I wrote candidly about the process that the LORD was taking me through. And I wrote down many goals and plans for the future. Over the years since my release, periodically I've gone back and looked at these pages. Here is what has happened: God has accomplished my written goals and plans and exceeded them in abundance. I never dreamed of the ministry that He has blessed me with, or the marriage that Micah and I have, or that He would restore my life to the point of having four grandkids that I love so much. God has given back more than a double portion of what the enemy has stolen.

> *"Now to Him who is able to do exceedingly abundantly above all that we ask or think, according to the power that works in us, to Him be glory in the church by Christ Jesus to all generations, forever and ever. Amen" (Ephesians 3:20, 21).*

It says "above all that we ask or think"; that's an amazing statement. I mean... we can ask and think for great things. God says..."Go ahead... I will do greater things than these." *Our God is an awesome God!*

One more thing that God does when He takes us into the wilderness is prepare us for the future. He may use the wilderness experience to prepare us for some type of Kingdom work. Let me give you two great examples:

The first example is the Apostle Paul. Most of us know about Paul's conversion on the road to Damascus, but what many don't realize is that after he received his sight back, Paul went into the wilderness in preparation for the work God had for him.

> *But when it pleased God, who separated me from my mother's womb and called me through His grace, to reveal His Son in me, that I might preach Him among the Gentiles, I did not immediately confer with flesh and blood, nor did I go up to Jerusalem to those who were Apostles before me; but I went to Arabia, and returned again to Damascus. Then after three years I went up to Jerusalem to see Peter and remained with him fifteen days. (Galatians 1:15-18)*

Why did Paul have to go into the wilderness? To unlearn the things that he thought he knew, because he had been raised in a very religious environment. God had to break him of his religious spirit; his self-righteousness. And then the LORD began the refining process, the transformation process; He began preparing Paul for his future work of the ministry. I've thought over the years what it would have been like to be a witness to Paul's wilderness experience. Paul went on to write 13 books in the New Testament. In studying his writings, one can discern the Holy Spirit's handprint all over Paul.

> Jesus called Paul... *"a chosen vessel of Mine to bear My name before Gentiles, kings and the children of Israel. For I will show him how many things he must suffer for My name's sake" (Acts 9:15, 16).*

The last and greatest example of the wilderness experience is our Lord and Savior Jesus Christ. Jesus had just been baptized and was preparing for His ministry. He also had to be tempted in all the ways that we are so He could relate to us in all areas. Both Matthew and Luke record Jesus's wilderness experience.

First let's look at Matthew's account...

Then Jesus was led up by the Spirit into the wilderness to be tempted by the devil. And when He had fasted forty days and forty nights, afterward He was hungry. Now when the tempter came to Him, he said, "If You are the Son of God, command that these stones become bread." But He answered and said, "It is written, 'Man shall not live by bread alone, but by every word that proceeds from the mouth of God.'" Then the devil took Him up into the Holy City, set Him on the pinnacle of the temple, and said to Him, "If You are the Son of God, throw Yourself down. For it is written: 'He shall give His angels charge over you,' and 'In their hands they shall bear you up, lest you dash your foot against a stone.'"

Jesus said to him, "It is written again, 'You shall not tempt the LORD your God.'" Again, the devil took Him up on an exceedingly high mountain, and showed Him all the kingdoms of the world and their glory. And he said to Him, "All these things I will give to You if You will

*fall down and worship me." Then Jesus
said to him, "Away with you, Satan!
For it is written, 'You shall worship the
LORD your God, and Him only you shall
serve.'" Then the devil left Him, and
behold, angels came and ministered to
Him." (Matthew 4:1-11)*

This is an amazing section of Scripture and over
the years I have done many teachings from these
verses. But for our discussion on the wilderness,
allow me to make some observations.

First: please take note that it was the Holy Spirit
who led Jesus out into the wilderness. Also, notice
that this event took place immediately after Jesus
was baptized. Obviously the entire reason that
Jesus came to earth in human flesh was to save
those who would believe in Him. But here the LORD
took Jesus out into the wilderness to prepare Him
for the next three years of His ministry. Jesus led a
perfect life, but He had to be tested and tempted as
we are so that He would be able to help us...

*"For in that He Himself has suffered,
being tempted, He is able to aid those
who are tempted" (Hebrews 2:18).*

As I mentioned; the LORD takes us into the wilderness to prepare us for a work that He may have
in store for us.

Next: it says that after Jesus fasted for forty days
and nights, He was hungry. Then the devil said
to Him; "*If* You are the Son of God"...see the word
there, "if"? The devil knew exactly who Jesus was,
but he was trying to plant a seed of doubt in His

mind. And the devil does the same thing to us. He's called the accuser of the brethren. He tries to get us to doubt who we are, to question our salvation.

And then he said to Jesus, "Command that these stones become bread." Jesus had been fasting for forty days... he was hungry... and so the devil tried to tempt Him at his place of weakness. "You're hungry... turn these stones into bread." The devil does the same with us... he tempts us at our place of weakness... is your weakness pornography? The devil will attack you there... is your weakness drugs... he'll attack you there... is your weakness money... he'll use that against you. Our enemy is real; he's smart and he's ruthless. This is a battle that we're in.

> *"Put on the whole armor of God, that you may be able to stand against the wiles of the devil" (Ephesians 6:11).*

That word "wiles" in the Greek is *methodeia*, which means "strategy, scheme, or lie in wait". The devil strategizes against us and we are called to put on the "armor of God" to withstand him.

Next: Jesus gives us a "key" in overcoming the enemy. When the devil tries to tempt Jesus at His place of weakness; Jesus responds with, "It is written"...please stop and make a "life note" here. *(This is very important.)*

Jesus says, *"It is written."* He could have done away with Satan right there, but He didn't. Instead Jesus said, "It is written..." Now stop and think about something – if Jesus quoted the word of God to the devil as His weapon of defense, doesn't it make sense that we should do the same? I have what I often refer to as my "warfare" verses that I go to when the devil tries to attack me. For example...

> *"No weapon formed against you shall prosper" (Isaiah 54:17).*

> *"If God be for us, who can be against us?" (Romans 8:31)*

> *"He who is in you is greater than he who is in the world" (1 John 4:4).*

...do you see what I'm doing here? When I know that the devil is attacking, with Jesus as my example, I say "as it is written" and I start quoting Scripture, just like Jesus did. The Bible is my weapon. In that section of verses from Ephesians about putting on "the whole armor of God", the only weapon mentioned is in verse 17 when it says, "take the sword of the Spirit, which is the word of God."

Why would anybody go into battle without a weapon? The simple answer is that we wouldn't. I repeat: the Bible is our weapon. That's one of the reasons the devil wants to deceive people into believing the Bible is no longer relevant. Without the word of God, we have no weapon to battle with.

Next: It's interesting what happened next in the exchange between Jesus and Satan. In verse six the devil says...

> *"If You are the Son of God, throw Yourself down. For it is written: 'He shall give His angels charge over you,' and 'in their hands they shall bear you up, lest you dash your foot against a stone.'"*

Notice: the devil says, "For it is written." Are you kidding me? Take a note, the devil is quoting Scripture to Jesus Christ. Do you see the audacity here, the boldness of the devil? He knows no limit to the extent to which he will attack. We have to be aware of the schemes of the enemy of our souls. Not only is he a liar, he is also a perverter of the word of God. The devil will take a verse of Scripture and twist it. That's why we have to study.

> *"Be diligent to present yourself approved to God, a worker who does not need to be ashamed, rightly dividing the word of truth" (2 Timothy 2:15).*

I will comment on Jesus's wilderness experience more in a later chapter, but let me conclude here by simply stating that our Lord and Savior was led into the wilderness in preparation for His ministry and to give us insight as to how we should respond. The Bible says...

> *"Submit to God. Resist the devil and he will flee from you. Draw near to God and He will draw near to you" (James 4:7, 8).*

That is what God wants to happen in the wilderness. He want us to submit, to surrender our lives fully to Him... and we will have to resist the attacks from the enemy while we're there because he *will* attack... but as we draw near to God, He will draw near to us.

I want to finish this chapter with a section of Scripture that speaks about the wilderness times in our lives:

Oh, give thanks to the LORD, for He is good! For His mercy endures forever. Let the redeemed of the LORD say so. Whom He has redeemed from the enemy, and gathered out of the lands, from the east and from the west, from the north and from the south. They wandered in the wilderness in a desolate way; they found no city to dwell in. Hungry and thirsty, their soul fainted in them. Then they cried out to the LORD in their trouble, and He delivered them out of their distresses. And He led them forth by the right way, that they might go to a city for a dwelling place.

Oh, that men would give thanks to the LORD for His goodness, and for His wonderful works to the children of men! For He satisfies the longing soul, and fills the hungry soul with goodness. Those who sat in darkness and in the shadow of death, bound in affliction and irons— because they rebelled against the words of God, and despised the counsel of the Most High, therefore He brought down their heart with labor; they fell down, and there was none to help. Then they cried out to the LORD in their trouble, and He saved them out of their distresses.

He brought them out of darkness and the shadow of death, and broke their chains in pieces. Oh, that men would give thanks to the LORD for His goodness, and for

His wonderful works to the children of men! For He has broken the gates of bronze, and cut the bars of iron in two. (Psalm 107:1-16)

I would encourage everyone reading this book to meditate on these verses...

God is good... His mercy endures forever... we who have been redeemed should say so... we were in the wilderness because we rebelled against the LORD and His word... yet when we cried out to Him; He redeemed us... He broke our chains... He freed us from bondage... He brought us out of darkness... He has broken the gates... He has cut the bars of iron... give thanks to the LORD... He is good!

We need to get to the place where we can say... "Thank You Father for the wilderness experiences. Have Your way with me... in Jesus's name, amen."

Chapter 7

Brokenness: God's Sweet Spot

—ɯ—

In discussing the subject of "brokenness", I find this to be one of the most misunderstood concepts in the church and with Christians in general.

The word "brokenness" invokes all sorts of negative connotations, many of which are not accurate in God's Kingdom. The enemy wants to paint all kinds of horrible pictures in our minds when we hear the word "brokenness". The devil doesn't want us to know about being broken because he wants to keep us in bondage. He doesn't want us to tap into the power, the freedom and the blessings of truly being broken.

The truth is that if we had any idea of the blessings tied to brokenness, we would pray for it, we would even seek it.

In this chapter, my desire is to clear up some of these misconceptions. I want to share my testimony of being broken and hopefully, convey to you that we do *not* have to fear it. As a matter of fact, we should ask the LORD to break us over and over again in our lives.

As I've done in previous chapters, I will apply the concept of brokenness to us as individuals and as a nation. It begins with individuals, but when we apply the concept of brokenness to a larger group, it can explode into a spiritual revival.

Almost every great revival began with a few people praying from the place of brokenness, then the LORD used that to ignite a spark, which in turn began to spread; then, as the Holy Spirit moved, that spark exploded into revival and whole nations were transformed. If there was ever a time for a people to recognize the need for revival in a country it would be now; it would be here, in the United States of America.

Let me make a bold statement: without a move of the Holy Spirit in America, without a revival in our country and soon, we in this great land of ours will witness the demise of our nation. Our *only* hope in this country, at this time in our history, is *Jesus Christ!*

The Concept of "Brokenness"

When I explain the concept of brokenness it begins with one word: "humility".

Over and over again through the Scriptures we see a consistent theme: God hates the spirit of pride and He has compassion for the spirit of humility.

Look at these verses:

> *God resists the proud, but gives grace to the humble. Therefore submit to God. Resist the devil and he will flee from you. Draw near to God and He will draw near to you. Cleanse your hands, you sinners; and purify your hearts, you double-minded. Lament and mourn and*

weep! Let your laughter be turned to mourning and your joy to gloom. Humble yourselves in the sight of the Lord, and He will lift you up. (James 4:6-10)

"For You do not desire sacrifice, or else I would give it; You do not delight in burnt offering. The sacrifices of God are a broken spirit, a broken and contrite heart. These, O God, You will not despise" (Psalm 51:16, 17).

Do you understand? We have it all backwards. The world has it all backwards. So, the first place to start in talking about the concept of brokenness is to understand humility. Is it too much to ask for you and me to simply admit that we don't have all the answers to life's problems? I know that I certainly don't and neither do you. Sometimes I don't even know the questions to ask, much less have the answers. I have mentioned before Proverbs 16:25, which says...

"There is a way that seems right to a man; but its end is the way of death."

I challenge you that not only does that apply for an individual, but also a nation. Left to our own devices, sometimes we make poor choices. A humble attitude says, "God is smarter than I am and I need Him to help me with my life." Many of us (I'm preaching to the choir here) have had a really difficult time with humility. We think humility is either a sign of weakness, or it represents low self-esteem. Both of these are misconceptions. A humble spirit is to be greatly desired by anyone who wants real spiritual growth; for anyone who wants a deeper walk with the LORD. And for a person to get to the place of brokenness, many times the LORD has to do it for us because we have a rebellious spirit.

Our human nature is to fight against being broken at all costs. Allow me to paint you a picture: We've all seen movies of wild horses before, how beautiful they are, but until a horse is broken, that horse can't be ridden or worked. That horse is useless for any kind of service until it is broken. The horse has to be broken and once it's broken, it can then be useful to its owner. The term of breaking a horse used to be called "to meek" the horse. I love that analogy. The word "meek" is a great word, which means "power under control". We've all admired the raw power and beauty of a stallion. But to use that stallion, he has to be broken; that power has to be brought under control. Then that horse can be used to do great things. This is a great word picture of being broken. Just as that stallion, we must be brought under control, so we can be used by our Owner to do some great things for His Kingdom. The two words "humble" and "meek" are very closely associated. In the Beatitudes, Jesus said...

> *Blessed are the poor in spirit, for theirs is the kingdom of heaven.*
>
> *Blessed are those who mourn, for they shall be comforted.*
>
> *Blessed are the meek, for they shall inherit the earth.*

Blessed are those who hunger and thirst for righteousness, for they shall be filled. (Matthew 5:3-6)

See the words "poor in spirit", "mourn", "meek". They all represent humility. Then see "hunger and thirst for righteousness". A person can't "hunger and thirst for righteousness" without first being humble. The proud, the arrogant, the haughty don't care about righteousness because they think they're righteous. All these traits Jesus mentions here are associated with humility.

Notice something else: there is a *blessing* tied to all four of these conditions. Then in verse 12 Jesus said...

"Rejoice and be exceedingly glad, for great is your reward in heaven."

Uh... Excuse me, Jesus... did You just say, "Great is your *reward* in heaven?" That's correct. There are not only blessings, but also rewards associated to humility. Now stop for a second and let that sink in... There are *blessings*... and there are *rewards*... tied to humility. With that in mind, why would anyone *not* want to have a humble spirit? Yet, in the world we live in today, humility is almost a bad word. As I mentioned before, if we had any idea the blessings tied to brokenness, we would not run from the experience, we would seek it and ask for it.

The next part of brokenness: truth.

The LORD wants us to come to the place where we are honest with Him in every area of our lives. Think about this: God already knows everything, so why not just go ahead and tell Him about it? As a parent, have you ever asked your child a question that you already know the answer to? Maybe they've done something that you found out about, so you ask them a question knowing the answer. Why did you ask them? To see if they would tell you the truth. Better yet... wouldn't you really want your child to come to you before you even asked and tell you? That's a picture of our heavenly Father. And if your child had come to you in the first place and said, "I need to tell you about something..." wouldn't that have been a blessing to know that they felt like they could come to you? Again, a picture of our heavenly Father. And if your child made a mistake, or did something wrong and they came and told you about it, even if you had to discipline them for it, wouldn't you still be glad they came and told you about it? And in making that mistake, you don't love them any less, do you? Again... a picture of Him. You just want your kids to be honest with you and come to you and that's what our Father wants as well. He can handle the truth... He's God.

> "Behold, You desire truth in the inward parts. And in the hidden part You will make me to know wisdom" (Psalm 51:6).

Through the process of brokenness that the LORD took me through, these were two key ingredients, "humility" and "truth". I've mentioned before that I had a spirit of pride that had been instilled in me as an athlete. I was the star on most of the teams that I played on; the captain of almost every team. That spirit of pride had spilled over into every area of my life. So for me, the pride had to be dealt with and God certainly did that. For a star athlete, raised in a good family, with everything going for himself in life, is there anything more humbling than to lose it all and ultimately go to prison? I can tell you that I was completely humbled. And I've already shared that I had to stop lying to my family, friends, myself and of course, to God. For me: God began the process of breaking me by allowing me to be arrested and go to prison.

The next part of brokenness: coming to the end of ourselves.

At the start of this chapter I said that we have negative connotations associated with the term "brokenness" that aren't accurate in God's kingdom and yet I talk about going to prison as part of the process God used to break me. While this sounds like a contradiction, it's not. This sounds crazy, but I have many fond memories of my time in prison and here's the reason for that.

I came to the end of myself: I came to the realization that no one else could save me, that I couldn't save myself and that it was just me and the LORD.

When we realize, through being humbled and admitting the truth, that the only hope we have left is Jesus Christ, we have arrived at the place of brokenness. It's at the place of brokenness that we cry out to God for His presence, His mercy, His love and His touch. For me: true brokenness brought me to the place where I realize that everything up to that point in my life was insignificant in comparison to what I was now experiencing. While I don't wish prison for anyone else, I wish that I could really convey the sweetness that true brokenness brings. Anyone that has experienced it knows exactly what I'm talking about. There really is a peace that surpasses all understanding. At the place where we are dead to ourselves, that's where you'll find the LORD. When we seek the LORD with all our heart...

I know the thoughts that I think towards you, says the LORD, thoughts of peace and not of evil, to give you a future and a hope. Then you will call upon Me and go and pray to Me, and I will listen to you. And you will seek Me and find Me, when you search for Me with all your heart. I will be found by you, says the LORD, and I will bring you back from your captivity. (Jeremiah 29:11-14)

This is one of the Scriptures that God used to change my life. Notice that God's thoughts are of peace and not evil. Also, that He wants to give us a future and hope. As a matter of fact: *He is our future and our hope!*

But also take note that we find Him when we search for Him with ALL of our hearts. God's doesn't want half our hearts or even most of our hearts. No, God wants *all* of our hearts. When Jesus told the rich young ruler in Luke...

"You still lack one thing. Sell all that you have and distribute to the poor, and you will have treasure in heaven; and come, follow Me" (Luke 18:22).

Jesus didn't care about the young man's money. This was a gut check. Jesus knew that this man's money was the most important thing in His life. Jesus was basically saying to this young man, "If there is anything that's more important to you than Me, then I'm not interested."

I have said this many times... "Jesus wants to be LORD of all, or He won't be LORD at all." That's what it means when it says "we find Him when we search for Him with *all* of our hearts."

I can't overemphasize this point: at the place of brokenness, we come to the realization that *nothing* – I repeat – *nothing* can or will come before Jesus Christ! Listen to this...

> *"He who loves father or mother more than Me is not worthy of Me. And he who loves son or daughter more than Me is not worthy of Me" (Matthew 10:37).*

These words were spoken by Jesus Christ Himself. They are strong words from our Lord about who is to come first in our lives.

Allow me to point out one of the things that I've experienced over the years in ministry. I meet men and women who put their children or grandchildren or their husbands or wives before the Lord. It is absolutely wrong; I don't know how else to say it. Please hear me: there can be no one, there can be no thing, that can come before Jesus Christ. Period. When Micah and I first met, I told her that she comes before me and everybody else, except for Jesus. And I told her to never to put me before Jesus. If some of you hearing this have been guilty of allowing your children, grandchildren, spouse or anything else to be first place in your life, then I am asking you to confess and repent of it. Tell the Lord you're sorry that you've done this in the past and ask Him to change your priorities to what they should be. I repeat... Jesus must be first in our lives ...it's non-negotiable!

While I was in prison there were a few things that happened that were instrumental in changing my life. Let me share one of those things here.

When I first arrived in prison, the Holy Spirit began the practice of waking me in the middle of the night. I would awake and begin reading and studying the word of God. This habit continues to this day and these are some of the greatest times for me spiritually. There is something precious about spending time with the LORD in the middle of the night... it's quiet; it's still and it's a wonderful time of fellowship with God. Moses, Abraham, David, Jeremiah all had a habit of rising early before dawn to spend time with our heavenly Father. And as always, our greatest example, Jesus, often rose early before dawn to spend time with the Father...

> *"Now in the morning, having risen a long while before daylight, Jesus went out and departed to a solitary place; and there He prayed"* (Mark 1:35).

This habit of rising in the middle of the night to spend time in prayer and study of the word has been a *key* in changing my life. When the Holy Spirit wakes me, I absolutely know it's Him.

On the morning of April 25, 2001 I awoke at 3:30 AM. The reason that I know the time is because I wrote it down in my Bible. I was in a tank (a large jail cell) with 53 other inmates. As I woke up, in my head was flashing "ISAIAH 43:10... ISAIAH 43:10... ISAIAH 43:10!" over and over again, like a neon sign. I was on my bunk and I always slept with my Bible by my head. So I rolled off my bunk onto my knees and began to pray. As I prayed, that verse continued to flash. I knew quite a bit of Scripture by this time, but as I knelt there I couldn't recall Isaiah 43:10 and it was really bothering me. So finally I reached over, took my Bible and opened it to ISAIAH... and here is what I read...

> *"You are My witnesses," says the LORD, "and My servant whom I have chosen, that you may know and believe Me, and understand that I am He. Before Me there was no God formed, nor shall there be after Me. I, even I, am the LORD, and besides Me there is no Savior." Isaiah 43:10, 11*

(Will you please read that again... very slowly?)

Now, will you try to imagine for a moment the scene here... an inmate... a prisoner... on his knees... in the middle of the night... reading these words... staring at these words for a long time... reading them over and over again.

I thought... *"What am I supposed to do with this, LORD?"* I wasn't able to go back to sleep that night. This is one of my "life" verses that the LORD used to break me. These words absolutely rocked my world. I was dumbfounded.

After meditating on this Scripture for years, allow me to share with you some of the things the Holy Spirit has taught me...

First: "You are My witnesses," says the LORD.

Wait a second... see that first word, "You"? ...LORD, are You talking to me? You can't be talking to me... Craig... I'm in prison... for breaking the law... You can't be talking to me! I've mentioned that I personalize the Scriptures and this is where it started. This was when I began to realize that

God will take anybody He wants to and use them anyway He chooses because He can... He's God. Here I am, a convicted felon and God says..."You are My witness." Talk about an overwhelming thought!

I thought, well, it says "witnesses" ...it's plural... so it's not talking specifically about me. The problem with that thought is the next sentence says, "and My servant". Uh ...it's singular... So – "Yes Craig... I'm talking to you." Ok... "LORD, You want me to be a witness?"

"Yes... a witness."

"To what?"

"Don't worry about all that right now... just know that you are to be a witness for Me."

"Ok LORD, but I don't know what You want me to witness about."

"Don't worry about all that right now."

"Ok, LORD".

Now, stop and think, what does a witness do? They tell what they've seen, what they've heard and they tell the truth. Wait... we're *supposed* to be witnesses, aren't we? Jesus said...

> *"You shall receive power when the Holy Spirit has come upon you; and you shall be witnesses to Me" (Acts 1:8).*

That's what we're supposed to do...

Allow me to point out something obvious here: God never does things on accident. And when God says something, He CAN and WILL fulfill it. Because...

> *"God is not a man that He should lie. Nor a son of man, that He should repent. Has*

He said, and will He not do? Or has He spoken, and will He not make it good?" (Numbers 23:19).

Ok... so, call me crazy... but this sounds as though the LORD is telling me that I am to be a witness for Him. "That's good Craig... you're starting to get the idea." Ok LORD. What's next?

Second: "And My servant whom I have chosen."

Again, talk about overwhelming. But then... all through the Bible God takes the most unlikely of characters and turns them into His vessels. Moses murdered a man; Noah got drunk; David was an adulterer; Jonah was a complainer and Saul/Paul was responsible for how many deaths? Now... not that I'm any one of those heroes in the Kingdom of God, but my point again is that God can take anyone He wants to and do what He chooses to... because He's God. But the word "chosen" really bothered me. Then I felt like the LORD said, "Can I not choose who I want?"

"Ok, LORD... but what am I supposed to do with that?"

"I said don't worry about all that right now."

"...Yes, LORD."

Third: "That you may know and believe Me, and understand that I am He."

This is an amazing sentence. There are three "key" words here:

1) the word "know"

This word in the original Hebrew language is the word *yada* and our English language doesn't do it justice. This word has a very deep meaning. It means: "to discern"; "to perceive in an intimate manner"; "to comprehend and consider with respect" and it denotes a very personal intimacy. This is not referring to a casual way of knowing someone, but of a deep intimate love towards a spouse or loved one. This means really, really, knowing someone, spending time with them, listening to their innermost thoughts and desires. Grasp the depth of this word. This is the same Hebrew word in Psalm 46:10,

"Be still and know that I am God."

2) the word "believe", which is the Hebrew word *aman*

It means: "to be trustworthy"; "to build up"; "to support"; "to foster as a parent"; "to be firm and faithful"; "to be permanent"; "fathering"; "to be certain". All that in that word? Yes. Also, notice something else: Who does it say to believe? God says "believe *Me*", not believe Me and... Oprah, or Me and Dr. Phil... or Me and anybody else... no, it says "believe Me"! God wants us to believe *Him*! That may sound insignificant, but it's not. *It's huge!*

3) the word "understand", which is the Hebrew word *bin*

It means: "to separate mentally"; "to distinguish"; "to learn, to think and discern intelligently"; "to inform".

Now, go back and read that sentence again: "That you may *know* and *believe me* and *understand* that I am He." The fact that God uses these three words together here in reference to who He is cannot be overstated. I repeat... this is an amazing sentence! I have spent many hours meditating on these words... and the more I do; the more in awe of Him I become.

Fourth: "Before Me there was no God formed, nor shall there be after *Me*."

When I began to really search the Scriptures and dig into God's word; I was amazed at the clarity. God leaves no room for any doubt. There is only One God and He's the God of Abraham, Isaac and Jacob, the God of Israel and there is *no other* God. Now, this would sound narrow-minded – if it wasn't true! I hear people say that it's awfully narrow-minded to claim that Jesus Christ is the *only* way to get to heaven. Once again, it would be if it wasn't true.

I may not be the smartest person walking around, but starting in Isaiah 43:10, listen to these verses:

> *"Before Me there was no God formed, nor shall there be after Me."*

> *43:11 "Besides Me there is no Savior."*

44:6 *"Thus says the LORD, the King of Israel, and his Redeemer, the LORD of hosts: 'I am the First and I am the Last: besides Me there is no God.'"*

44:8 *"You are My witnesses. Is there a God besides Me? Indeed there is no other Rock; I know not one."*

45:5 *"I am the LORD, and there is no other; there is no God besides Me."*

45:6 *"That they may know from the rising of the sun to its setting that there is none besides Me. I am the LORD, and there is no other."*

45:14 *"There is no other God."*

45:18 *"I am the LORD, and there is no other."*

45:21 *"And there is no other God besides Me, a just God and a Savior; there is none besides Me."*

45:22 *"For I am God, and there is no other."*

46:9 *"Remember the former things of old, for I am God, and there is no other; I am God, and there is none like Me."*

Are there any questions here? How can anybody not understand that there is only *one God?* Eleven times in this section of Scripture, the LORD makes it starkly clear that there was never a God before Him; that He is the *only true God* now and that there will *never* be a God after Him.

Fifth: "Besides Me there is no Savior."

As I knelt there staring at these words for what seemed like hours... it was as if the LORD were saying to me...

"Craig: we can do this *My* way... or we can do this *My* way!" (That's *not* a typo.) "I AM GOD... there is *no* other God here or anywhere else for you to turn to. You can't save yourself and no one else can save you... I am your only hope here. The running is over, because I've got you locked up. The lies are over because there's no one left to lie to. It's just you and Me here Craig and I AM GOD; I AM the only Savior here!"

And that's when it hit me like I had been slapped across the face. *It's over. I'm done.* My life as I had known it... was over with. All the things that I thought I knew meant nothing... all the opinions that I had till then were nonsense... all the words that I had spoken to that point in my life were empty... my past actions, foolish... my past relationships, meaningless... my pride, a joke... my self-worth, gone... at that moment in time, at that place, in that prison cell, on my knees, *I was crushed. I was shattered.* I had nothing to say... nothing to offer... I couldn't move... couldn't get up off my knees... I was an empty shell of a man. *I was broken!*

This is what the concept of brokenness is about.

The title of this chapter is: "Brokenness: God's Sweet Spot".

You're probably thinking something like: "Craig, after what I've just read; why would I want to go *there*?" Here's why: let me give you a word picture that I feel as though the Holy Spirit, just now, as I am writing this, gave me. We all have experienced as a child the fear that strikes us when a parent tells us that we're getting ready to have to take medicine. Or the fear that strikes many of us even now when we think of having a needle stuck into us at the doctor's office. *It's going to hurt.* That's right: it *is* going to hurt; there will be some pain involved; it won't be pleasant. But, if we're sick, we take the medicine to get well. We know that the pain involved will ultimately help us to heal. That's a great picture of the brokenness experience. There will be some pain involved. Sometimes it *hurts*. It's fearful and we resist it at all costs. But the after effects are *so* worth it...

> *"Now no chastening seems to be joyful for the present, but painful; nevertheless, afterward it yields the peaceful fruit of righteousness to those who have been trained by it" (Hebrews 12:11).*

Does that say "peaceful"? Yes, "peaceful". Does that say "righteousness"? Yes, "righteousness". Does that say "fruit"? Yes, "fruit". I want peace; don't you? And I mean real peace. I want my life to bear fruit, don't you? And I want to live my life right before God; don't you? These are the traits that God wants for us as well.

Our heavenly Father always has our best interest in mind and He sees the end from the beginning. If I would have been able to see what my life looks like now from the day that I was arrested, I would have tried to bargain with God to see if there was any way to get here without the process of brokenness. But the LORD is all knowing. He knows what's best for us and sometimes that involves going through some pain that left to ourselves, we wouldn't choose. My Father in heaven loves me enough that He had me arrested, put in prison and then He broke me behind those walls. Sounds strange, doesn't it? But...

> *"'My thoughts are not your thoughts, nor are your ways My ways,' says the LORD. 'For as the heavens are higher than the earth, so are My ways higher than your ways, and My thoughts than your thoughts'"* (Isaiah 55:8, 9).

Many times God's ways are actually opposite our ways. I don't wish prison for anyone; but that's what it took for me to get still and to come to the understanding that He is God. And as I look back on my time in prison, I can tell you without any hesitation that was the greatest time of my life because that's when I got "born again" and the LORD began the process of transforming my life.

Now... let me make mention of the process of brokenness in relation to an entire nation. As a concerned American, I find that both political parties are ripe with corruption. The greed, lies and outright corruption are rampant in our nation and exist in every level of government. I live in a suburb of Dallas and it grieves me tremendously that in the last few years we have witnessed leaders in the Dallas Independent School District and city government go to jail for stealing, fraud and other corruption charges. You may say that it goes on in every city and that's just the way things are done, but that is exactly my point. When I grew up, I believed that government officials were supposed to be the cream of the crop, the leaders in the community and we expected them and trusted them to conduct themselves with the highest morals and values. Is that too much to expect from our leaders? I say, "No, it's not."

This corruption is at the city, state and national levels. And the really sad thing is that we have the officials that WE elected. They are a representation of us, the people. I hear people say that we weren't really formed as a Christian nation, but they are mistaken. I have studied this to settle it in my own mind; and I can tell you without a doubt that America was formed as a Christian nation.

I can also tell you that our nation today is very much like the nation of Israel was during the time when the LORD prophesied through Jeremiah. The nation of Israel was wealthy, powerful, had been blessed by God and all other nations knew that; and slowly they began to turn away from the LORD. God used the prophet Jeremiah to warn the leaders and the people that if they would simply acknowledge that they had turned away, repent and turn back to Him, they would be ok, but if they did not turn back to Him they would be destroyed...

> *I brought you into a bountiful country, to eat its fruit and its goodness. But when you entered, you defiled My land and made My heritage an abomination. The priests did not say, "Where is the LORD?"*

And those who handle the law did not know Me; the rulers also transgressed against Me; the prophets prophesied by Baal, and walked after things that do not profit. (Jeremiah 2:7-9)

Notice that the LORD here speaks about the spiritual leaders when He says "priests" and "prophets", then He addresses the law makers (politicians) when He says, "those who handle the law did not know Me." He then addresses what would be business leaders today when He says, "the rulers also transgressed against Me." So... here we have the spiritual leaders, politicians and business leaders all together. Doesn't that sound like America today?

Our spiritual leaders have grown soft. They have compromised the word of God and been silent far too long and far too often about the direction of our nation. On key topics of national importance the church has grown silent.

I love that the word of God so directly states, "Those who handle the law did not know Me." If our national leaders in Washington knew the LORD, they would not put into place laws that go directly against God's word. And they would not be so arrogant to overturn other laws that are in line with the word of God. The corruption and the mishandling of the nation's financial resources are tragic. Ask this question: where is the fear of the LORD in Washington today?

And then we have our business leaders. I remember growing up and my father told me: "If a man's handshake isn't any good, then the man isn't any good." And "If a man's word is no good, then he's no good." My, how far we've slid. What has happened to the word "integrity" in conducting our day to day affairs?

I've made mention of the fact that in my life I came to the realization that there were consequences for the choices and decisions that I made. And those principles apply not only to individuals, but also to a nation. When a nation that has been *so* blessed by God (as we have been here in America) turns away from Him, there will be consequences. And just as the LORD uses the process of brokenness to do a deep work in an individual's life, He will also do to a nation, to bring that nation back to Him. We, as a nation, are at a crossroads. I do not believe our greatest threat is terrorism or the economy. I believe our greatest threat is that we as a nation are morally and spiritually destroying ourselves from within. Listen again to a few verses from Jeremiah...

> *Has a nation changed its gods, which are not gods? But My people have changed their glory for what does not profit... For My people have committed two evils: they have forsaken Me, the fountain of living waters and hewn themselves cisterns (wells) – broken cisterns that can hold no water...*

> *Have you not brought this on yourself, in that you have forsaken the LORD your God when He led you in the way...Your own wickedness will correct you and your backslidings will rebuke you. Know therefore and see that it is an evil and bitter thing that you have forsaken the*

LORD your God, and the fear of Me is not in you," says the Lord God of hosts. (Jeremiah 2:11-13,17,19; commentary added.)

We as a nation have turned from the LORD and put our trust in politicians, the economy, our own selves and allowed the devil to lead us astray in the name of tolerance. We have turned from the only true God that there is – the God that blessed us for so long – and we've lost the fear of the LORD, the reverential respect towards Him that keeps us humble and obedient to His word. And so: just as the LORD will use the experience of brokenness for an individual, He will also use that brokenness to bring us back to Him as a nation. I believe God has begun to remove His hand from America. How long and how far we drift into the wilderness is up to us. He will allow us to continue down the road we've chosen as far as we choose to go. But just like the nation of Israel did over and over again, at some point, when we confess our sin of turning from Him and when we repent and return to Him, He will then forgive our sin as a nation and He will heal our land. We can't heal our land on our own and we can't fix all our problems or we would have done it by now. Only He can. At this time in our nation's history, our *only* hope is Jesus Christ!

To summarize: it's at that place of brokenness where we come to the realization of who we are. That our human nature is sinful. We get a clear perspective on our sin and then we're able to get a clear understanding of who God is. That He is a Holy God. That He is a righteous God. And at that point we totally surrender to His power, His Glory,

His Majesty and we admit that we don't have the answers to life's problems, only God does.

One of the reasons brokenness is so sweet is because when we are truly broken, our heavenly Father doesn't leave us there. The Bible says...

"The goodness of God leads you to repentance" (Romans 2:4).

God is good... and all His ways are right. And at the point of brokenness; He can begin the process of reshaping us, of remolding us. I was just starting to get an understanding of what that meant...

"LORD, You alone are worthy... the fact that You didn't give up on me and that You don't give up on us as a nation speaks about Your goodness, Your patience and Your love. Thank You Father for not giving me what I deserved. And thank You for not giving us what we deserve as a nation. I need Your mercy and we need your mercy. We've sinned against You, LORD. So Father, I ask in the name of Jesus, that You would turn us back to You and create in us an attitude of humility and a spirit of repentance for ever turning from You. Personally LORD, I thank You for loving me enough to break me when I needed it. I pray that we as a nation will not come to our ruin before we wake up and return to You. LORD, we need spiritual revival in our nation today. We need Your Holy Spirit to fall upon us as a people and ignite in us a fire for You. Help us to trust in Your word again and to live our lives in obedience to Your word again. Please God, move upon us... touch us... and do not remove Your hand of protection and blessing from America. Bring us back to Jesus... and let Your Kingdom

112

come on earth as it is in Heaven. All these things I ask and pray in Jesus's name; amen."

Chapter 8

The Potter's Wheel

—ᗰᗰ—

At the place of brokenness I was an empty vessel. I had come to the realization that I had nothing to offer a Holy God. That's why Isaiah said at his place of brokenness...

> "Woe is me, for I am undone! Because I am a man of unclean lips, and I dwell in the midst of a people of unclean lips; for my eyes have seen the King, the LORD of hosts" (Isaiah 6:5).

When I first read this verse I thought: "Now wait a second, we're not talking about just anybody here. We're talking about Isaiah... I mean "me", a man of unclean lips? Yes, definitely... Or "you", a person of unclean lips? Yes, definitely... Who of us doesn't stumble in speech sometime, someway? But, this is *Isaiah!* This is "the prophet" as he was known. Jesus quoted Isaiah. So... what's up? Was Isaiah having a problem with his language in some area?

No... what happened to Isaiah happens to all truly broken people. He came to the place where he saw God as He really is. Isaiah said..."My eyes have seen the *King, the Lord of Hosts."* Isaiah realized he was nothing in the presence of Almighty God. He had nothing to offer God. He was broken before God... and that's why he said..."Woe is me, for I am undone."

The term "woe" was a legal term that meant, "I am dead" or "I am guilty." And the word in Hebrew for "undone" is the word *dama*, which means "ruined" or "to be silenced".

At my place of brokenness I was "ruined", "silenced", "guilty"; I was "dead" to myself. And that's exactly where God wanted me to be. At this point the Holy Spirit led me to my next "life" Scripture...

> *The word which came to Jeremiah from the LORD, saying: "Arise and go down to the potter's house, and there I will cause you to hear My words." Then I went down to the potter's house, and there he was, making something at the wheel. And the vessel that he made of clay was marred in the hand of the potter; so he made it again into another vessel, as it seemed good to the potter to make. Then the word of the LORD came to me saying: "O house of Israel, can I not do with you as this potter?" says the LORD. "Look, as the clay is in the potter's hand, so are you in My hand, O house of Israel!"* (Jeremiah 18:1-6)

Let me share what the Holy Spirit has taught me over the years about this section of verses...

First: Notice that it says..."go *down* to the potter's house, and there I will cause you to hear My words."

115

So... my question is why do we have to go *down* in life to hear the words of the LORD? Why can't we hear the words of the LORD when everything is going great? Our human nature is that when things are going great, most of us don't really seek the LORD. We're too busy enjoying the good times or taking credit for our own success to stop and pursue God. And that's a shame, isn't it? Unfortunately for most of us, it's when we have a tragedy in our lives that we cry out to God. Let me give you an example. After 9/11, there were record numbers in church attendance... for *two* weeks – and then the numbers were back to normal. *Tragic.* It's when we lose something precious to us or fall on hard times that most of us seek God. Why, when something happens, does prayer seem to be the last resort for many of us instead of the very first thing we do? I am a witness that most of us have to go *down* to hear the word of the LORD. It shouldn't have to be that way, but the fact of the matter is that's the way it usually is.

Next: It says, "The vessel that he made of clay was marred in the hand of the potter."

That word "marred" in the Hebrew is the word *sabat*, which means "ruined, corrupted, flawed, or wasted". That's a perfect description of me. I was ruined, flawed, corrupted and my life had been wasted. If you've ever seen a potter making a vessel of clay, if that vessel has a crack in it, or a flaw in it, the potter can't just slap a piece of clay on there. No; if the vessel is flawed, the potter must smash the clay and start over again. He must remake the vessel. That's what it means here when it says, "So he made it again into another vessel, as it seemed good to the potter to make." I was marred and my

Potter had just smashed me so He could remake me again into another vessel, as it seemed good to Him to make.

Next: I've mentioned that I personalize the Scriptures; and in the next two verses when it says, "O house of Israel", I inserted my name and you can insert yours here as well. It says, "Then the word of the LORD came to me, saying: 'O Craig Nedrow, can I not do with you as this potter?' says the LORD. 'Look, as the clay is in the potter's hand, so are you in My hand, O Craig Nedrow!" Here is another verse that explains that God is the Potter...

> *"But now, O LORD, You are our Father; we are the clay, and You our potter; and all we are the work of Your hand"* *(Isaiah 64:8).*

Can not the potter do as He wishes with the clay?

> *"Shall the clay say to him who forms it, 'What are you making?'" (Isaiah 45:9).*

> *"But indeed, O man, who are you to reply against God? Will the thing formed say to Him who formed it, 'Why have You made me like this?' Does not the potter have power over the clay, from the same lump to make one vessel for honor and another for dishonor?" (Romans 9:20, 21).*

Let me state this as clearly as I know how. God is God and He can do what He wants, with who He wants and He really doesn't owe you and I an explanation. And the sooner many of us come to that realization, the better off we would be. That's also a fact that helped me when He began the process of making me into another vessel that seemed good to Him.

It's at the place of brokenness that God can begin to form us into a vessel that will be useful for His Kingdom purposes. Remember that I said earlier, when God breaks us, He never leaves us like that. He begins the process of reshaping us into the image of His Son Jesus Christ. (Now, just as a footnote, once we are on the potter's wheel, we'll never get off of it, at least not on this side of Heaven.)

> *"Being confident of this very thing, that He who has begun a good work in you will complete it until the day of Jesus Christ"* *(Philippians 1:6).*

Now that God had broken me, He had just begun His good work in me. Now began the process of changing me from the inside out. Notice that it's God that does the good work in us. The clay has nothing to do with what the potter is preparing. Sometimes we think that the potter needs our assistance. The fact is, we've already messed things up badly enough that we had to be broken, so what we need to do is stay out of the way and let God do the work. I can take no credit for the person that God has made me into today. He's not done yet, but I can tell you that anybody that knew me before and knows me now will tell you that I am a different person than I was before.

Over the years since I got out of prison, the LORD has opened so many doors for me to be a witness about how Jesus Christ changed my life. And one of the areas that has really struck me and grieved me is the area of other addicts in their recovery process and I would like to comment on this subject.

The reason that I want to comment about this is because I care about people and I see so much devastation in the lives and families of people who have an addiction, whatever that addiction may be. Please hear what I'm about to say from a place of concern, not criticism.

I am such a small percentage of people that have been delivered from years of drug addiction. As I watch others who struggle with different addictions, whether it be drugs or alcohol or pornography or whatever it may be, I am saddened by the rate of relapse, the lack of real victory over these addictions. I have spent time praying about this very subject and this is what has been revealed to me.

There are so many 12 step programs out there with really low numbers of success. I have met so many people that have been in rehab after rehab after rehab and 12 step after 12 step and the question that begs to be asked is: "Why is there so little victory over these addictions?" Please, again, I'm not trying to be critical of these programs, but really, why can't we get more people well? Here's what I have discovered.

In most of these programs we refer to: "A higher power as you know it"... Wait a second; what is *that?* "A higher power as you know it"? I believe the devil laughs at that. He loves it when we don't give it a name. That higher power as you know it could be anything. It's like taking a knife to a gunfight. We need to take the gloves off. We need to stop worrying about offending everybody and start getting people healed. My so called "higher power" has a name and

His name is Jesus Christ! I say... let's call upon the name of Jesus and let's get people well. I get angry about this because I see so many people that are in bondage to the devil through their addictions and yet we're more concerned about offending somebody than we are about getting people set free.

"Therefore if the Son makes you free, you shall be free indeed" (John 8:36).

The title of this book is: "Free Indeed" and this is where the title came from. This Scripture startled me the first time that I really read it and let it sink in. Now put this in context of all the people with addictions. If we believe the Bible is true (and I do) and it says here that Jesus can "make you free, and you shall be free indeed", then why wouldn't we want to do that? And you may say to me: "Craig, if it was just that easy, we would do it." I get that. And you would be right in a way. If it was just reading one verse from the Bible and getting set free; but that's not what I'm talking about here. A few verses previous to John 8:36 it says...

"Then Jesus said to those Jews who believed Him, 'If you abide in My word, you are My disciples indeed. And you shall know the truth, and the truth shall make you free'" (John 8:31, 32).

Two quick points here:

First: It says "to those Jews who believed Him". That's a crucial statement – *to those who believed Him.* Our approach to the word of God is absolutely critical in any healing process. Will you read the word with a doubting heart or with a believing heart? If you choose to be a skeptic when studying the Bible, you won't receive the blessings from the word of God.

"If you will not believe, surely you will not be established" (Isaiah 7:9).

Second: Do you see the word "abide" in that verse? That word means "to dwell" or "to sit down and remain". That's important because we need to dwell in the word of God; to sit down and remain in the word of God. There is something called "The Big Book" that the 12 step programs use and to work the program a person has to spend time studying the big book. Well, what I am saying is, here is *the Book of books*. If I told you that if you would study *this* Book (the Bible) and believe this Book and put the principles found in this Book to work in your life, you would absolutely be healed from any addiction, would you *not* want to do that? Well, that's exactly what I am telling you. And the reason that I can say that with authority is because I'm a witness that it will work.

I was an addict for 20 years and couldn't stop on my own. When I went to prison, I started spending countless hours reading and studying and meditating on God's word and I believe God's word. And in the process I came to know the truth and the truth made me free. I never had to go through a 12 step program or a rehab program.

Jesus Christ redeemed me from my addiction and He can redeem anyone. But why am I such a small percentage of those that really do get redeemed from

121

addictions? I believe it's because most people aren't ready to *totally* surrender their lives to Christ. You may disagree with that and that's ok, but I have watched many people closely for several years to come to that conclusion. For whatever reason, most people just aren't ready to totally surrender. This may offend some, but I can't help that. I would say, "Don't get offended; get surrendered and get healed."

Notice also, it doesn't say there: "Therefore if your higher power as you know it makes you free, you shall be free indeed."

Until we stop kidding ourselves and start calling on the name of Jesus, we're never going to see true freedom for addicts and others who are in bondage. You may be saying: "Who made you the expert, Craig?" I'm no expert; what I am is a witness. As the song says, "I was lost, but now I'm found; I was blind, but now I see." I don't know of any other way to say it: Jesus Christ set me free from years of drugs. It's not a day to day struggle, I don't fight cravings, I don't have to go to meetings to stay clean and sober because "the Son made me free, and I am free indeed." I have been redeemed from years of drugs because, just like Job said...

"I know that my Redeemer lives"
(Job 19:25).

I said all that to say this: these programs put the focus on *our* efforts to overcome. They say things like; "Work the program." It's about *our* work that we are putting into it. Instead, we need to come to that place of submission to Jesus Christ and allow Him to heal us. We can't fix ourselves. Only Jesus can fix us.

That's why when we get broken and allow God to be the potter, He will begin that process of changing us, of fixing us, of reshaping us. Our responsibility is to surrender to Him. He's the potter, we're the clay. Allow God to be God. Allow the Master Potter to take the clay and do what He wants to do and stand back in amazement at what He makes.

Us as a Nation

Back in Jeremiah 18, God speaks about the potter's wheel on a national level beginning in verse 7...

The instant I speak concerning a nation and concerning a kingdom, to pluck up, to pull down, and to destroy it, if that nation against whom I have spoken turns from its evil, I will relent of the disaster that I thought to bring upon it. And the instant I speak concerning a nation and concerning a kingdom, to build and to plant it, if it does evil in My sight so that it does not obey My voice, then I will relent concerning the good with which I said I would benefit it.

Now therefore, speak to the men of Judah and to the inhabitants of Jerusalem, saying, "Thus says the LORD: 'Behold, I am fashioning a disaster and devising a plan against you. Return now every one from his evil way, and make your ways and your doings good.'" And they said, "That is hopeless! So we will walk according to our own plans, and we will

> *every one obey the dictates of his evil*
> *heart." (Jeremiah 18:7-12)*

I remember the first time that I read these verses; I wept for my nation. Jeremiah was known as the "weeping prophet" and I understand why. His nation had been called God's chosen people and they still are, but how it broke Jeremiah's heart to watch his nation drift away from the LORD. And today my heart breaks for my nation as I witness the same thing.

I would like you to notice that how a nation responds to the potter has a direct effect on what happens next to that nation. We see here that as the Potter begins His process, if that nation does evil there will be disaster and if that nation does good, then God will relent of the disaster. Verse 10 specifically says... "if it does evil in My sight so that it does not obey My voice". So let me ask a question here. Does God still expect a nation to "obey His voice"? I can tell you without any hesitation that He does...

> *"I am the LORD, I do not change"*
> *(Malachi 3:6).*

How arrogant we are in America to think that God's word no longer applies to us, that somehow things are different now and so we no longer need to abide by His word. Who would God be if He destroyed Sodom and Gomorrah for their sexual perversion and wickedness and yet didn't bring judgment on us? And then I hear people say, "Yes, but that's in the Old Testament and we live in the age of grace under the New Testament." Well then, let's look at what the New Testament says...

> *For if God did not spare the angels who sinned, but cast them down to hell and delivered them into chains of darkness, to be reserved for judgment; and God did not spare the ancient world, but saved Noah, one of eight people, a preacher of righteousness, bringing in the flood on the world of the ungodly; and turning the cities of Sodom and Gomorrah into ashes, condemned them to destruction, making them an example to those who would afterward would live ungodly; and delivered righteous Lot, who was oppressed by the filthy conduct of the wicked. (2 Peter 2:4-7)*

> *"As Sodom and Gomorrah, and the cities around them in a similar manner to these, having given themselves over to sexual immorality and gone after strange flesh are set forth as an example, suffering the vengeance of eternal fire" (Jude 7).*

Both these verses are from the New Testament and both use the sin of sexual perversion as "an example". Now, if God judged an entire region for the sexual perversion and disobedience of the people then and says in the New Testament that they are set forth as examples for those who would come after them, do you see the dangerous position we have put ourselves in here in America?

It's amazing to me that people believe that the judgment of God couldn't happen to our nation. There are those who believe that it has already begun. I believe that God *has* begun to remove His hand of protection from our nation and He is watching to see how we will respond. Will we confess that we've turned away from Him, repent of our sin and return to the LORD and in turn avoid His full judgment, or will we choose to say as they did there in Jeremiah 18:12 "So we will walk according to our own plans, and we will every one obey the dictates of his evil heart"? America can fall and we will fall if we don't humble ourselves to God Almighty.

What happens in America is up to the people of America and the leaders of America, but without a doubt we are at a crossroads. If we return to the LORD, we will continue to be a blessed nation, but, if we continue down the same road that we're on now, we will be destroyed as a nation. I am sure of that.

The potter's wheel is where the LORD begins the process of reshaping us. We must come to the clear understanding that there is a Potter and there is the clay. And the Potter is the LORD and we are the clay.

"Father, how gracious You are and have been to us. We have a choice to make. We can either submit to You as the Potter, or we can rebel to You and suffer the consequences of our choices. I ask You in Jesus's name that You would help us to confess, repent and return to You. I ask in Jesus's name that people would come to the understanding that You have our best interests in mind, both individually and as a nation. LORD, have mercy on us, not because of who we are, but because of who You are. Thank You for loving us as we are. In Jesus's name, amen."

Chapter 9

Transformation: The Process Begins

—ɰ—

When we hear the word "transformation" many thoughts may come to mind, so let me begin this chapter and give you the word picture for what I mean when discussing "transformation". Merriam Webster describes "transform" as: a) to change in composition or structure; b) to change the outward form or appearance of; c) to change in character or condition; convert; d) to cause to undergo genetic change and the act of "transformation" as "the act, process, or instance of transforming or being transformed". That's actually a great description of what the Lord did and continues to do in me. He changed my character, my condition, my outward appearance; He converted me and actually went back and did a genetic makeover in me. Now, if that sounds like a massive project, it was and as I said, He is still in the process.

> *"Being confident of this very thing, that He who has begun a good work in you will complete it until the day of Jesus Christ" (Philippians 1:6).*

127

That verse is exactly what God does: He begins the good work and then He will continue it until His Son returns and brings us home.

I mentioned in the last chapter that once we're on the Potter's wheel, we will never be done this side of Heaven. I am a witness of this as well.

I have heard others say there is no such thing in the Christian life as just staying the same. We are either continuing to grow or we are allowing ourselves to fall away. I don't totally agree with this statement. As a matter of fact, I see many people who aren't growing, but aren't falling away. They just seem to be in a rut mode where they love the LORD, but they're not growing. And in my opinion this is a very dangerous spot to be in, because if we're falling away we usually are aware of it and can stop the fall. And if we're growing, we know the LORD is working in us. But when we're in the rut mode – that stagnated place – we can become numb and ineffective for the Kingdom of God and the devil loves it when he has a Christian in that place. It's almost like the devil says, "Look, I know you're saved, but I don't want you on the battle lines witnessing and testifying so just sit down on the bench over there and shut up." We become ineffective for the Kingdom. If this is where you're at, get ready because God won't allow you to stay there too long before He will shake things up and you'll feel the Potter's hand again.

Now that the LORD had broken me, He wasn't going to leave me there. I knew that I was on the Potter's wheel and I had no idea what was in store for me. But I knew that He had a lot of work to do.

Once the Potter gets the basic shape, He can then begin the process of smoothing the clay; giving the clay its distinct features and preparing the vessel to show. The Potter also has to put the vessel into the hot furnace to harden it. Then, He also has to polish the vessel before it's ready for showing.

In the transformation process the Lord literally changed everything about me. I don't know what I expected, but the change has included my speech, my mind, my morals, my value system, my attitudes, my physical body, my future life experiences and of course my eternal destiny. Allow me to share with you part of what my Father in Heaven has and is continuing to do.

1. He changed my speech.

One of the very first things that the LORD did with me in the transformation process was that He changed my speech. I had a real problem with profanity. And overnight that was gone. I just didn't swear anymore. I find it interesting in Isaiah 6 after he says that his eyes have "seen the King, the LORD of hosts" the very next thing that happens is...

> *"One of the seraphim flew to me, having in his hand a live coal which he had taken with the tongs from the altar and he touched my mouth with it, and said: 'Behold, this has touched your lips, your iniquity is taken away, and your sin is purged'" (Isaiah 6:6, 7).*

The angel touched Isaiah's mouth with a live coal and his sin was taken away. The coal represents purification here. The LORD had chosen Isaiah for service and now He began to prepare him. I am going to discuss this purification more in detail, but before moving on to that I want to comment further on the speech issue.

As we see and as I mentioned, one of the first things the LORD does is to deal with our speech. This is very important for several reasons. As a Christian, we are called to be different from the world. Simply put, there should be something different about us that creates a curiosity from others to want what we have. Maybe I am even more sensitive to this because I used to speak so badly, but doesn't it sound horrible when someone who confesses to being a Christian begins to use profanity? I mean, it's like fingernails on the chalk board. While none of us is perfect in every area of our speech, we should make it a very high priority to watch our language. Most of us wouldn't use profanity in church, or if we were having a conversation with our pastor, so why would we think it's right when we're out in the world? As a matter of fact, shouldn't we be just as careful when we're out in the world because that's where we are supposed to be representing Jesus? The unbelieving world watches Christians very closely and sadly, many times they see people who aren't any different from themselves. Jesus called us to be "salt and light" and that means we're to be noticeably different...

> *"'Come out from among them and be separate,' says the Lord. 'Do not touch what is unclean, and I will receive you. I will be a Father to you, and you shall be My sons and daughters,' says the LORD Almighty"* (2 Corinthians 6:17, 18).

How we speak *is* important. It's simply not a good witness for someone who claims to be Christian, but his or her speech is peppered with profanity.

The LORD also changed my speech in the area of exaggerating and lying. When we totally surrender our lives to Christ, the Holy Spirit dwells within us and what happened to me next was profound. I can't remember where it happened the first time, but I remember that I said something and it was as if the LORD tapped my on the shoulder and said, "That's not true, so stop doing that." It kind of startled me. The LORD changed me in this area.

I want to be a man of my word. I also want to be a man of integrity. I may not be perfect, but I want to honor the LORD with my speech. When I say something, I want to do everything possible to do what I say. We all know people who will say... "I swear to God this and that" ...and my question here is.. .if you don't say "I swear to God", does that mean that everything else you say is a lie? Listen to what Jesus said about this...

> *"I say to you, do not swear at all: neither by heaven, for it is God's throne; nor by the earth, for it is His footstool; nor by Jerusalem, for it is the city of the great King. Nor shall you swear by your head, because you cannot make one hair white or black. But let your 'Yes' be 'Yes' and your 'No' be 'No'. For whatever is more than these is from the evil one."* (Matthew 5: 34-37)

Our words are important to Jesus and He wants us to know it. It caused me to pause and really think about my speech when I came across the following words of Jesus...

> *"I say to you that for every idle (means careless) word men may speak, they will give account of it in the day of judgment. For by your words you will be justified, and by your words you will be condemned" (Matthew 12:36, 37; commentary added).*

These are sobering words from our Lord and Savior. There are entire books about how important our words are and obviously I can't do a detail study on that here. But let me make mention of another area that I think is worth noting.

I am taken back by the sheer arrogance of people today, as I'm sure many of you are as well. The lack of humility is apparent in our world today and it's sad. In the book of James we get a word about this arrogance...

> *Come now, you who say, "Today or tomorrow we will go to such and such a city, spend a year there, buy and sell, and make a profit;" whereas you do not know what will happen tomorrow. For what is your life? It is even a vapor that appears for a little time and then vanishes away. Instead you ought to say, "If the Lord wills, we will live and do this or that." But now you boast in your arrogance. All such boasting is evil. (James 4:13-16)*

Since I first read this, the Lord has seasoned me in the area of arrogant speech. I really try to include "Lord willing" in my speech when I talk about what I may be trying to do.

The bottom line is, we should pray for wisdom, asking the Lord to help us with our speech. While we won't be perfect, we should be conscious of how we talk and we really need to grasp the fact that we are representatives of Christ here on earth. We are called to be different and our speech *is* very important. I am grateful to the LORD for the work He has done in the area of my speech and I want to continue to grow in this area.

2. Next, he changed my mind.

I can't overemphasize the importance of the mind in the process of transformation. The mind is where the devil attacks. This is a crucial area the Lord changed in me. The classic example of Scripture about the mind is...

> *"Do not be conformed to this world, but be transformed by the renewing of your mind, that you may prove what is that good and acceptable and perfect will of God" (Romans 12:2).*

This is an amazing verse: first; it tells us to "not be conformed to this world"; the word "conformed" means "to be molded to" or "shaped like" and it paints the picture of a cookie cutter forming a piece of dough. I was a great example of someone who had been conformed to the world for many years.

Think about something: we take in information all day long from T.V., the internet, movies, the radio and almost all of it is pure garbage. We are literally bombarded with junk, filth and information designed to manipulate us and, as we speed through our day, most of us are simply oblivious to it. With that in mind, it is absolutely crucial that we renew our minds with something good. Think of it this way: if an athlete eats pure junk food all day long, they won't be in top shape. What they eat is very important, so they have a strict diet. Now, apply the same concept to our spirit. We cannot feed our spirit junk all day long every day and expect it not to have a profound effect upon us.

Next, it says to "be transformed' and we've already looked at what "transformed" means. Now notice it says "by the renewing of your mind", so let's talk about the "renewing" part. Let me give you three keys for renewing the mind.

First Key: Prayer.

Through prayer, we must have the help of the Holy Spirit to renew our minds.

Jesus said in John 14:26 that "the Helper, the Holy Spirit, whom the Father will send in My name, He will teach you all things, and bring to your remembrance all things that I said to you."

Without the Holy Spirit, my life would not have changed. The Holy Spirit is my Teacher, my Counselor, my Comforter, my Corrector, my Power and without Him I could not live the Christian life. So, in prayer, ask to Holy Spirit to renew and cleanse your mind daily. Ask the LORD for a fresh infilling of the Holy Spirit every day. It can't be overemphasized how crucial it is that we surrender to the Holy Spirit and allow Him to do His work in renewing our minds.

Second Key: The word of God.

We have to feed ourselves on the word of God if we are to grow spiritually. With all the junk that I mentioned that our minds are bombarded with, the word will cleanse us, show us the truth and help us to discern between good and evil. Listen to two verses:

> *"You are already clean because of the word which I have spoken to you." Jesus said this in John 15:3.*

The word of God cleanses us as nothing else can. In my transformation process, the word has and continues to be the cleansing tool that the LORD uses. I love the word of God. I am a student of the word. I love to study the Greek and the Hebrew to deepen my understanding of the word. And every day before I spend time in the word, I try to pause and ask the Holy Spirit to teach me what He wants me know. Remember John 14:26, "He will teach you all things." My teacher is the Holy Spirit and He needs to be yours as well.

> *For though by this time you ought to be teachers, you need someone to teach you again the first principles of the oracles of God; and you have come to need milk and not solid food. For everyone who partakes only of milk is unskilled in the word of*

*righteousness, for he is a babe. But solid
food belongs to those who are of full age,
that is, those who by reason of use have
their senses exercised to discern both
good and evil. (Hebrews 5:12-14)*

Obviously, the word of God is the food here. If we
are to grow spiritually, we must feed on God's word.
And yet, there are so many Christians that are literally starving from lack of spiritual nourishment.
If a baby isn't fed, they won't grow and the same
applies to our spirit.

Notice also that it says in this verse that the word
is how we are able to "discern both good and evil".
Let me ask you a question: how are we to discern
between good and evil without a guide? Where is
our plumb line to test what's good and evil? Are we
going to base that on what the world says? Because
that's the wrong place to go for counsel. Or, are we
going to take counsel from a day time talk show?
To me, this is a no brainer. I need Godly counsel
and I need to get it from the word of the living God.
When we hear something, we should go to the Bible
and see what it says. If it doesn't line up with God's
word, then it's wrong. That may sound drastic, but
we are living in drastic times. The word of God is
absolutely essential in the process of renewing our
minds. I can't over state this.

Third Key: We must have firewalls on what
we take in.

In the renewing of the mind; we have to not only
feed on the good, but guard against the filth that is so
rampant in our world today. For example, in my car

I listen to almost exclusively Christian radio. I watch sermons and listen to sermons on a regular basis. I read Christian books when I'm not reading the Bible. And I put strict guards on what I allow my eyes to see.

> *"I have made a covenant with my eyes; why then should I look upon a young woman?" (Job 31:1).*

> *"I will set nothing wicked before my eyes; I hate the work of those who fall away; It shall not cling to me. A perverse heart shall depart from me; I will not know wickedness" (Psalm 101:3, 4).*

> *"How can a young man cleanse his way? By taking heed according to Your word" (Psalm 119:9).*

Do you see a pattern here? It takes discipline, but the rewards are so worth the effort.

Let me give you another reason that the mind is so important. I stumbled upon this years ago and I have meditated and prayed about it for a long time. In the book of Deuteronomy we see the great commandment that was given to the people of God...

> *"Hear, O Israel: the LORD our God is one! You shall love the LORD your God with all your heart, with all your soul, and with all your strength" (Deuteronomy 6:4, 5).*

Now, in Mark 12 Jesus quoted these verses from Deuteronomy, but I noticed something very interesting...

137

"Hear, O Israel: the LORD our God is one!
You shall love the LORD your God with
all your heart, with all your soul, with all
your mind, and with all your strength.
This is the first commandment" (Mark
12:29, 30).

Please pause and take notice that Jesus added
"with all your mind". Now, we know that Jesus never
made a mistake, so He must have had a reason for
adding "the mind". I believe that Jesus was looking
down the corridors of time and knew that it would
become increasingly more difficult, especially in the
last days, for people to love Him with all their mind.
When I stop and think of all the distractions that
we're assaulted with mentally, the Holy Spirit led
me to Daniel 12...

"But you, Daniel, shut up the words, and
seal the book until the time of the end;
many shall run to and fro, and knowl-
edge shall increase" (Daniel 12:4).

That word "increase" means "to explode" or "to
increase exceedingly". Statistics tell us that in the
year 1900, knowledge doubled about every 125
years; by the year 1925 it was down to about every
50 years; by the year 2000 it was down to about
every 3.5 years and in the year 2012 knowledge
doubles every 18 months. Estimates are that by
2020 knowledge will double every 30 days! With
all the technology at our disposal, loving the LORD
with "all our minds" takes discipline and our priorities must be focused to avoid being led astray. Once

again, this is where the help and power of the Holy Spirit must be present in our lives.

Please listen to me: there is nothing more important than spending quality time in prayer, serious study of the word of God and we must feed our spirits with Godly thoughts and information and then guard our eyes, ears and hearts. These are very serious days we are living in. I am so grateful that the LORD has changed me in the area of my mind. However, I understand that the renewal of the mind is an ongoing process.

3. He changed my morals.

This was an area that the LORD opened my eyes to that has truly been life changing. The definition of moral is: "of or relating to principles of right and wrong in behavior; ethical behavior; conforming to a standard of right behavior."

> *"There is a way that seems right to a man, but its end is the way of death"* *(Proverbs 14:12).*

> *"He who walks in his uprightness fears the LORD, but he who is perverse in his ways despises Him"* *(Proverbs 14: 2).*

> *"The fear of the LORD is the beginning of knowledge, but fools despise wisdom and instruction"* *(Proverbs 1:7).*

Can you imagine my situation? Here I am in prison for my stupid choices in life and the Holy Spirit shows me these verses. I immediately confessed my sin of my morals and repented of all my years of rebellion against the LORD. This was another part of the brokenness that God took me through. For years I lived my life independent from the LORD and did whatever I wanted to do, without a second thought about other people and about right living.

I mentioned before that I believe one of the main problems in our nation today is that we've lost the fear of the LORD. If our leaders had a true fear of the LORD, they would govern differently and our nation wouldn't be in the position we're in today. When we hear the term "fear of the LORD", the word "fear" means a "reverential awe" and "respect" for the LORD. While we do need to fear Him in the real meaning of the word fear, that word means *so* much more than our English language allows us to comprehend.

Once again: I can't overstate the power of God's word in my life. Listen to this...

> *"Your word is a lamp to my feet and a light to my path" (Psalm 119:105).*

> *"Your word I have hidden in my heart, that I might not sin against You" (Psalm 119:11).*

The entire 119th Psalm is about the word of God. Let me recommend to anyone reading this book: quality time spent in the 119th Psalm will have a profound effect on your daily walk with the LORD.

I would also like to make one more recommendation, the book of Proverbs has 31 chapters. A person can read a chapter of Proverbs in less than five minutes. This is a great starting place to feed yourself spiritually each day. Ask yourself, when and where can I consistently fit in five minutes a day for what I urge is the most important five minutes you'll spend that day. I can testify that if you will read chapter 1 on day 1, chapter 2 on day 2 and so on throughout a 30 or 31 day month and repeat this same practice each and every month, it will have a serious effect on your moral behavior. Proverbs is a window into our spirit on how to live a successful Christian life. Ask someone who has incorporated this habit of reading a chapter a day of Proverbs into their lives and listen to what they will tell you. All I am saying is five minutes a day and you'll be shocked at the positive results. Please try this; you won't regret it.

Just as I mentioned our speech as Christians, our moral behavior is just as important. How we live our day in and day out lives is so important to the unbelieving world that is watching us. It is a sad fact, but when a well-known Christian figure takes a fall, the unbelieving world rejoices in it. They love to watch and say, "See? Those Christians are just like everyone else, actually worse, because they act so high and mighty, but look at what just happened. What a bunch of hypocrites." And you know, they would be right in many instances. We as Christians aren't perfect, we're forgiven, but how we live our daily lives is very important. We should take our daily walk with the LORD very seriously. I will discuss this more in a later chapter.

Allow me to just tell you: if the LORD can take a rascal like me and change my moral behavior the way He has, then He can and will change anyone. To God be all the glory for the transformation He has done in me and continues to work in me morally.

4. He changed my value system.

This may sound like the same as my morals and they are closely related, but there is a foundational difference that is important to note here.

> *"Delight yourself in the LORD, and He shall give you the desires of your heart"* *(Psalm 37:4).*

Allow me to teach on this concept for a few minutes. People see this verse and focus on the last part of "He shall give you the desires of your heart" and God does want to do that. However, let me explain what many people fail to grasp here. When we surrender our lives to Christ, in the transformation process, God begins to change our hearts desires to line up with His desires for us and then He begins to grant us the desires of our heart. In my own life, things that used to be important to me no longer have the importance that they once did. And things that at one time were of no importance now mean something. The LORD realigns our priorities to match His priorities for us. In Matthew 6 Jesus was teaching the people not to worry about food, clothing and the such and He said...

> *"Seek first the Kingdom of God and His righteousness, and all these things shall be added to you" (Matthew 6:33).*

It also says in 1 John..."*Now this is the confidence that we have in Him, that if we ask anything according to His will, He hears us. And if we know that He hears us, whatever we ask, we know that we have the petitions that we have asked of Him" (1 John 5:14, 15).*

Notice that it says "according to His will". That is what I mean when I say that He will change our desires into His desires for us. When we pray, we should always ask, "according to Your will, LORD."

When we seek the LORD and put Him first, He has our best interests at heart and He knows what is better for us than we do because He's God. Many times people will pray for something only to not receive what they prayed for, but come to find out later that what the LORD had in mind for them was so much better than what they asked for. God's will is always the best for us if we will just trust in Him.

"Trust in the LORD with all your heart, and lean not on your own under-standing; in all your ways acknowledge Him, and He shall direct your paths" (Proverbs 3:5, 6).

As hard as it is to do, when we allow our values to be His values, our lives will be so much better. In my life, as the LORD changed my value system, the chaos that was so prevalent changed and there began to be peace in my life; things began to make sense and my life has been different ever since. What a blessing when we simply relax and allow God to be God and understand that His ways really are higher than our ways and His thoughts than our thoughts. I thank the LORD that He loved me enough to change my values to His values and then He began to give me the desires of my heart.

5. He changed my attitudes.

One of the areas that I needed the most transformation in was being self-centered. As an addict
and being single for most of my adult life led me
to think only about my own interests. Our attitude
towards others is very important to the LORD and
He has definitely changed me in this area. I had
never really stopped to consider the effect that my
actions had on those who cared about me the most.
And in my years of ministry since prison, I see that
this is an area that many people also fall short in.
We have become a very self-centered society and the
damage that has caused us as a nation is consid-
erable. What has happened to caring for our fellow
man in America? Listen to what the word of God
says in regard to this...

> *"Let nothing be done through selfish
> ambition or conceit, but in lowliness of
> mind let each esteem others better than
> himself. Let each of you look out not only
> for his own interests, but also for the
> interests of others" (Philippians 2:3, 4).*

> *"Be kindly affectionate to one another
> with brotherly love, in honor giving pref-
> erence to one another" (Romans 12:10).*

My, don't these verses humble us to think how
far we've slid as a nation? This was an area of my
life that I had to confess and repent of. My self-centered attitude had been a problem for many years,
but thanks be to God that by His grace and mercy
He has transformed me in this area.

Now, let me caution that the Bible is clear that as we continue to approach the return of Jesus, things will get increasingly worse in this area... Jesus said, speaking of the signs in the last days...

"Many will be offended, will betray one another, and will hate one another. Then many false prophets will rise up and deceive many. And because lawlessness will abound, the love of many will grow cold" (Matthew 24:10-12).

The spirit of arrogance and self-centeredness is rampant in the world today and will only get worse. This is just one more reason why we as Christians must spend quality time in the word of God. Without the word to correct and transform us, we will become more and more like the world.

I have to reflect daily on my attitude toward others. One of the things that help me to have the correct attitude towards others is to get outside of myself and help others. Doing things like helping the elderly, the less fortunate, feeding the homeless, or doing some type of charitable work takes the focus off ourselves and gives us a different perspective on life. If we are to grow spiritually, a servant attitude is essential. As always, Christ is our ultimate example of the attitude that our Father wants us to have.

"God resists the proud, but gives grace to the humble" (James 4:6).

In Luke 16 Jesus said... *"For what is highly esteemed among men is an abomination in the sight of God" (Luke 16:15).*

145

I am continuing to grow in the understanding that

"His thoughts are not our thoughts and His ways are not our ways; for as the heavens are higher than the earth, so are His ways higher than our ways and His thoughts than our thoughts" (Isaiah 55:8, 9).

Through the process of brokenness and the transformation that has followed, the LORD changed my attitude about myself, others and life in general. I realize that the world doesn't revolve around me. When we have Jesus Christ at the center of our lives, everything changes. Others become more important than us and life takes on a new meaning. A humble spirit is to be greatly desired in our walk with the LORD. Pray and ask the Holy Spirit to help you in the area of your attitudes.

6. He changed my physical body.

This may seem strange to you the reader that the LORD changed my body, but I am going to give you a life changing verse that astounded me.

Before I share this verse with you though, let me ask you a question. Do you believe in physical healing? The answer for most of you is probably "yes", so if we believe in physical healing, then wouldn't it also make complete sense that God could actually heal and restore the physical effects of years of drug abuse? I am a witness that God can and did restore my physical body.

We all have seen the pictures of the before and after shots of people who have been ravaged by years of drug use or cigarette smoking or drinking and how devastating the pictures can be. And those are just the physical appearances. The internal damage done through the abuse is just as severe. Damaged organs, other related illnesses and diseases from abuse are also a reality. And yet, with over 20 years of drug use, the lingering effects in my body are simply gone. There is no logical reason for this.

The truth is that the LORD has healed my body internally and externally, in addition to everything else that He has done in me. If we believe that the "word of God is alive and active" then listen to these verses...

"I am the LORD who heals you"
(Exodus 15:26).

"I have heard your prayer, I have seen your tears: surely I will heal you" (2 Kings 20:5).

"Have mercy on me, O LORD, for I am weak; O LORD, heal me, for my bones are troubled" (Psalm 6:2).

"O LORD my God, I cried out to You, and You healed me" (Psalm 30:2).

"Bless the LORD, O my soul, and forget not all His benefits: Who forgives all your iniquities, Who heals all your diseases, Who redeems your life from destruction, Who crowns you with loving kindness and tender mercies, Who satisfies your mouth with good things, so that

your youth is renewed like the eagle's"
(Psalm 103:2-6).

"He heals the brokenhearted and binds up their wounds" (Psalm 147:3).

"For thus says the High and Lofty One who inhabits eternity, whose name is Holy: "I dwell in the high and holy place, with him who has a contrite and humble spirit, to revive the heart of the contrite ones...I have seen his ways, and will heal him; I will also lead him and restore comforts to him and to his mourners" (Isaiah 57:15, 18).

"He was wounded for our transgressions, He was bruised for our iniquities; the chastisement for our peace was upon Him, and by His stripes we are healed" (Isaiah 53:5).

"Heal me LORD, and I shall be healed; save me, and I shall be saved, for You are my praise" (Jeremiah 17:14).

"For I will restore health to you and will heal you of your wounds, says the LORD" (Jeremiah 30:17).

"They brought to Him all sick people who were afflicted with various diseases and torments, and those who were demon-possessed, epileptics, and paralytics; and He healed them" (Matthew 4:24).

"Then Jesus said to the centurion, 'Go your way; and as you believed, so let it be done for you.' And his servant was healed that same hour" (Matthew 8:13).

"And great multitudes followed Him, and He healed them all" (Matthew 12:15).

"And when Jesus went out He saw a great multitude; and He was moved with compassion for them, and healed their sick" (Matthew 14:14).

"Jesus answered and said to them, 'Assuredly, I say to you, if you have faith and do not doubt, you will not only do what was done to the fig tree, but also if you say to this mountain, "Be removed and be cast into the sea," it will be done. And whatever things you ask in prayer, believing, you will receive'" (Matthew 21:21, 22).

These are what I have referred to as "my healing verses". These are verses that when I was in prison, I read over and over and over again and when someone that has come to me for Scripture about healing, these are the verses that I refer them to. These words *are alive!* And if we will read them and believe them and stand on them, then the LORD can heal us.

Now, let me share with you the life changing verse that I mentioned at the start of this section. I was in my cell in prison when the Holy Spirit showed me this; it was very late in the night and afterwards

I remained up the rest of the night dissecting and breaking it down. Here's the verse and then let's look at five key words in the Greek language that will bring this verse to life...

> *"But may the God of all grace, who called us to His eternal glory by Christ Jesus, after you have suffered awhile, perfect, establish, strengthen, and settle you. To Him be the glory and the dominion forever and ever. Amen" (1 Peter 5:10).*

Here are the five words and their Greek meanings and then we will read this verse once more with those meanings.

1) "suffered" = Greek *pentho*; means "to experience a painful sensation"
2) "perfect" = Greek: *katartizo*; means "to mend and restore"
3) "establish" = Greek: sterizo; means "to turn resolutely in a certain direction"
4) "strengthen" = Greek: *sthenos*; means "to give bodily vigor and spiritual power and knowledge"
5) "settle" = Greek: *themelioo*; means "to lay the foundation for"

Now... here's that verse with the Greek meaning inserted...

> *"But may the God of all grace, who called us to His eternal glory by Christ Jesus, after you have (suffered a painful sensation for a while, mend and restore you,*

turn you resolutely in a certain direction, give you bodily vigor, spiritual power and knowledge, and lay your foundation for) you. To Him be the glory and dominion forever and ever. Amen" (1 Peter 5:10). *'Commentary Added'*

Wow, is that an amazing Scripture! For so many of us that have suffered for so long, this is a life verse that if we could get ahold of could literally change our lives.

Please listen to what I am telling you: this was a revelation to me to know that God loved me enough and cared about me enough to mend and restore me; to turn my life around in a certain direction, to give me bodily vigor (that's the physical healing that I was speaking about), spiritual power and knowledge (The Holy Spirit) and then He would lay my foundation for my future coming out of prison. This verse shook me to the core when the Holy Spirit showed it to me. I don't have the words to express my gratitude or my devotion to the LORD for what He's done for me and in me.

The physical healing that the LORD has done in me is a miracle. I should have been dead by now with the amount of abuse that I put this body through. It is by God's grace and God's goodness and God's awesome healing power that I am alive and that I am as healthy as I am. Thank You Father! In Jesus's name! Amen.

7. He changed my eternal destiny.

Obviously, the most important thing that came out of the process of being broken by God was that

I was born again. There are no words that can be spoken that convey the joy and peace that comes from knowing that we will spend eternity with Jesus Christ and Almighty God as our Father in Heaven. To have our names written in the Lamb's Book of Life – there is nothing that can compare.

This is not a process; it was done the moment that I surrendered to Jesus as Lord and Savior of my life.

However, the process of sanctification is what begins at the moment we're born again. Sanctification is the process of becoming holy. It begins the moment we're saved and it will continue until we go home to be with the LORD or until Christ comes for His bride. It is God's will that we become holy...

> *"For this is the will of God, your sanctification" (1 Thessalonians 4:3).*

The process of sanctification can't begin until we've first been born again. But when we're born again, our destiny is changed from spending eternity in hell, separated from Jesus Christ and Father God to spending eternity in Heaven with our Lord and Savior and our Father God.

I can't make the choice for you, nor can anyone else. To be born again and have our names written in Lamb's Book of Life is a personal decision that every person must make.

> I want to *"implore you on Christ's behalf, be reconciled to God. For He made Him who knew no sin to be sin for us, that we*

might become the righteousness of God
in Him" (2 Corinthians 5:20, 21).

The transformation process that the LORD has begun in me is the greatest journey that anyone can have. And while I am not yet what I will be, I am not what I once was. Thanks be to God that He loves us enough to transform us through the process of sanctification into the children that He wants us to be...

> "Now the Lord is the Spirit; and where the Spirit of the Lord is, there is liberty. But we all, with unveiled face, beholding as in a mirror the glory of the Lord, are being transformed into the same image from glory to glory, just as by the Spirit of the Lord." (2 Corinthians 3:17, 18)

One last thought about the transformation process: when the LORD takes us through this process, He always has His Kingdom perspective in mind. The fact that we don't understand or agree with what He is doing in us doesn't change that we must trust Him and allow Him to be the Potter and realize that we are the clay and the clay doesn't tell the Potter what to do.

"LORD, thank You for the transformation process that you take us through to change us from glory to glory, changing us into the image of Your Son Jesus Christ. Continue this good work that You've begun in each of us until the day of Jesus's return. Help us to understand that You have our best in mind as You take us through this process. Have Your way with us. In Jesus's name, amen."

PROSPERITY SECTION

Chapter 10

No Turning Back

—ᴍᴍ—

Allow me to pause and do a quick recap. And the reason is because this chapter represents a real turning point in my life... up until this point most of the book has been focused on the "prison" section... the part of my testimony that has dealt with the correction, brokenness and transformation that the LORD has done and continues to do... but now we will transition into the "prosperity" section that will focus on the abundant life that Jesus spoke about...

> *"I have come that they may have life, and that they may have it more abundantly"* *(John 10:10).*

As a witness for Jesus, let me simply state: if I could get people to grasp the blessings tied to a life of total surrender, obedience and faith in Christ, we wouldn't need the rehab facilities, the anti-depression meds, the therapists and our nation wouldn't be in the position that we find ourselves in today. If this sounds like a radical statement, it's because I mean it to be a radical statement. Hear me clearly: Jesus Christ is our only hope individually and as a nation! He's the answer to a dying nation.

So... a quick recap...

I was a young man who had been blessed with tremendous gifts, such as:

Being born in one of the greatest, if not the greatest country in the history of the world...

A good family with loving parents and siblings...

Reasonable intelligence (very debatable) with an understanding between right and wrong...

Athletic abilities that opened doors of opportunity for me...

A middle class upbringing (not rich, not poor)...

Now...with a foundation such as this; I should have been well on my way to a successful life...

But in my late teens I began to make poor choices and there are consequences for our choices in life. Despite all the advantages that were part of my life... wisdom had not been one of them. As I reflect back, one of the essential ingredients in a young person's life that I did not have was Godly counsel. So, to a young person who may be reading this book, or a parent that would like to have their child read this book, take this advice to heart: Godly counsel is one of the most important things a young person needs in life!

This counsel should come from a trusted, grounded source who has Jesus Christ at the center of their life.

Very simply put...

> *"Where there is no counsel, the people fall"* *(Proverbs 11:14).*

As I began to make poor choices, they soon began taking me down the wrong path in life.

This may be difficult for some people to hear, but once past the age of accountability (which varies between young people), our father is either the devil, or our Father in Heaven. Jesus made this very clear when He said...

> *Why do you not understand My speech? Because you are not able to listen to My word. You are of your father the devil, and the desires of your father you want to do. He was a murderer from the beginning, and does not stand in the truth, because there is no truth in him. When he speaks a lie, he speaks from his own resources, for he is a liar and the father of it. But because I tell you the truth, you do not believe Me. Which of you convicts me of sin? And if I tell you the truth, why do you not believe Me? He who is of God hears God's words; therefore you do not hear, because you are not of God.* (John 8:43-47)

These are difficult words for most of us to grasp, but they were spoken by our Lord Jesus. And while they may be difficult to grasp, the fact that Jesus spoke them makes them true and relevant. Just as when He spoke this, people today have a problem with the truth that Jesus is the *only* way to get to Heaven. But do not be deceived; the devil is a liar and Jesus is the Truth.

Our father is either the devil, or our Father is God. Before I was born again, my father was the devil; he's a liar and so I had been lied to most of my life. I made bad choices in life, which took me down dark roads.

But God had a different plan for me. Out of His love for me, He arranged for me to be arrested and then sent to prison. At that point He took me out into the wilderness and there He broke me; I surrendered and then He began the transformation process. Notice that I said He began the process. He's the Potter; we're the clay.

The rest of this book is about the decision to "never turn back"; to move forward on the journey. We will discuss the importance of becoming obedient to the LORD and the blessings that are tied to that obedience. We will discuss the peace which truly surpasses all understanding, the walk of faith that we must all take and the joy and power that comes from the Holy Spirit's presence in our lives. We will also look at what the word of God says about growing in Christ, the need for courage in the world we live in today and about taking a stand for our faith. Finally, we'll look at the importance that prayer has in our lives.

There is an urgency that should burn in everyone who calls themselves a follower of Christ. We all have people we know who are not yet saved. While Jesus was clear that no one knows the hour or the day that He will return, He also said there would be signs that would signal His soon return. These signs have all taken place. Jesus Christ could come any moment. You may not agree with that, but I have spent thousands of hours studying the Scriptures. Christ is coming back, or the entire Bible collapses and our entire Christian faith is futile.

As we continue... let me share why I knew at this point in my life that there was...

No turning back...

When I speak in prisons and at churches, I emphasize that the battle really never begins until we surrender our lives to Christ. Up until that point we're no threat to the devil, because we're his children anyway. But once we've given our lives to Christ, now the devil is angry. I have had people tell me, "Once I gave my life to Christ, it seemed like all hell broke loose." And I say, "Well... welcome to the family."

The devil wants to discourage new believers from pressing forward. He wants to steal your joy, to kill your enthusiasm for your new life in Christ and to destroy your future destiny, because that's what he does.

But here's the deal... there is no turning back. Let me repeat that... *there is no turning back!*

Once we've surrendered our lives to Christ, there can be no going back and allow me to give Scripture support of that...

You have need of endurance, so that after you have done the will of God, you may receive the promise: "For yet a little while, and He who is coming will come and will not tarry. Now the just shall live by faith; but if anyone draws back, My soul has no pleasure in him." But we are not of those who draw back to perdition, but of those who believe to the saving of the soul. (Hebrews 10:36-39)

The endurance is needed because there will be attacks from the enemy. One of the things that many Christians seem to have either forgotten or never have grasped is that we are in a battle. This is spiritual warfare. The Bible teaches over and over that there is a battle between good and evil. Jesus never promised that after we surrender our lives to Him that everything would be easy. As a matter of fact, He said just the opposite...

If the world hates you, you know that it hated Me before it hated you. If you were of the world, the world would love its own. Yet because you are not of the world, but I chose you out of the world, therefore the world hates you. Remember the word that I said to you, "A servant is not greater than his master." If they persecuted Me, they will persecute you. If they kept My word, they will keep yours also. But all these things they will do to you for My names sake, because they do not know Him who sent Me. (John 15:18-21)

Jesus has told us that the world will hate us. Never in America did I ever think that we would actually experience this hatred toward Christians, but it's happening before our very own eyes. This breaks my heart for my nation.

These are strong words spoken by our Lord. And yet when Jesus says something will happen, it *will* happen. And things will only continue to get worse.

Remember: *there's no turning back...*

> *"You therefore must endure hardship as a good soldier of Jesus Christ. No one engaged in warfare entangles himself with the affairs of this life, that he may please him who enlisted him as a soldier"* *(2 Timothy 2:3, 4).*

Craig; I thought this was the beginning of the "Prosperity Section". What's all this warfare stuff? Let me answer that question for you...

We as human beings need to have a purpose in life. No one just goes through life without wanting to somehow make a difference. One of the best-selling books in recent memory was about a purpose-driven life. So... let me ask you a question.

Is there a higher calling than to be offered an opportunity to come alongside the Lord Jesus Christ and be part of His Kingdom army? I mean, pause for a moment and imagine Jesus saying to you...

"I am waging war against evil. We will win the victory. It's already guaranteed by My Father in Heaven. And in the process of winning, the reward is that billions of lost people will be saved. I am offering you a position with Me in My army. The battle will be difficult at times, but the reward will be beyond anything you could ever imagine. I will never leave you nor forsake you in this battle. This will be the greatest war in the history of mankind and the greatest victory in the history of mankind. I repeat, the outcome is already decided. Do you want to join Me in this fight?"

Are you kidding me? I am in!

Why can't we wrap our minds around this? How could we *not* want to be part of this? This is the highest calling there is, folks.

Over the years since I have become a student of God's word, I have developed such an admiration for the Apostle Paul. This man was a true warrior for Christ. At one point in his life, Paul said...

> *Brethren, I do not count myself to have apprehended; but one thing I do, forgetting those things which are behind and reaching forward to those things which are ahead, I press toward the goal for the prize of the upward call of God in Christ Jesus. (Philippians 3:13, 14)*

Paul had a clear understanding of what his purpose was. This was a man who had been an enemy of the Lord. He had been responsible for the persecution of many Christians. Before his name was changed to Paul, his name was Saul of Tarsus and he was zealous in his hatred for the early church of Jesus Christ. As I mentioned before with so many of us, his father was the devil and he had been lied to by the devil. And yet God chose Saul to be a vessel for His Kingdom purpose. Speaking about Saul on the road to Damascus, Jesus said this to a man named Ananias...

"But the Lord said to him, 'Go, for he (Saul) is a chosen vessel of Mine to bear My name before Gentiles, kings, and the children of Israel. For I will show him how many things he must suffer for My name's sake'" (Acts 9:15, 16; commentary added).

Here was an enemy of the cross and yet God chose him to be one of the greatest servants in the Kingdom of God. This is amazing to me. If God took Saul, changed his name to Paul, used him as a chosen vessel and then used him to write 13 books in the New Testament, then He can use someone like you and me for whatever purpose He chooses as well.

I have to tell you that as I sat in prison and began to really meditate on this concept of being in a war between good and evil, it began to have a deep and profound effect upon me. The Holy Spirit began to open my mind to the fact that not only had I been lied to, but that there is an enemy of our souls out there and he is more evil than we could ever dream. The world has painted this picture of some little red dragon with a pitchfork as the devil and nothing could be farther from the truth. People think that they can dabble in the spirit world of witchcraft, astrology, palm reading, the occult, tattoos and fortune telling and it not have an evil effect upon them. Wake up people! The spiritual realm is more real than the physical realm that we walk around in every day and the devil knows that his days are numbered. He is unleashing his army against God's saints and most Christians are completely oblivious to it.

While we don't have to fear the devil we absolutely need to be aware of who he is and what the stakes are...

> *My brethren, be strong in the Lord and in the power of His might. Put on the whole armor of God, that you may be able to stand against the wiles of the devil. For we do not wrestle against flesh and blood, but against principalities, against powers, against the rulers of the darkness of this age, against spiritual hosts of wickedness in the heavenly places. Therefore take up the whole armor of God, that you may be able to withstand in the evil day, and having done all, to stand. (Ephesians 6:10-13)*

This is a classic section of Scripture about spiritual warfare and I will discuss this later, but I want to focus here on the phrase "wiles of the devil". That word "wiles" in the Greek is *methodeia* and it means "strategies", "schemes" and "to lie in wait". That is a very descriptive word in the Greek language. The devil schemes against us, he strategizes against us, he lies in wait for those who he can devour. He is patient, he is clever, he is diabolical and as I said, he is more evil than any of us realizes. For this reason alone, we should understand that...

There's no turning back...

There is another very important reason that we can never turn back. And that reason is because, as I mentioned briefly at the start of this chapter,

Jesus *is* coming back soon. You may think this point gets too much attention, but since this event will be the climax of human history, we must talk about it often. Listen to the warning Peter gave us...

Beloved, I now write to you this second epistle (in both of which I stir up your pure minds by way of reminder), that you may be mindful of the words which were spoken before by the Holy prophets, and of the commandments of us, the apostles of the Lord and Savior, knowing this first; that scoffers will come in the last days, walking according to their own lusts, and saying, "Where is the promise of His coming? For since the fathers fell asleep, all things continue as they were from the beginning of creation." (2 Peter 3:1-4)

Listen people: we are in these days. Unbelievers and even many believers, think those of us who talk about being in the last days are just a bit crazy. I pray for spiritual discernment often. This is not a game we're playing here. The souls of many lost people are at stake. I don't care who thinks I may be crazy. Listen to these words of our Lord...

Whenever you see a cloud rising out of the west, immediately you say, "A shower is coming," and so it is. And when you see the south wind blow, you say, "There will be hot weather," and there is. Hypocrites! You can discern the face of the sky and of the earth, but

how is it you do not discern this time?
(Luke 12:54-56)

The signs are everywhere around us. If we would spend the quality time to study the word of God like we do other things that interest us, we would understand the seriousness of the time that we're living in. Past generations have dreamed about living in the days that we're living in now.

This is an amazing time to be alive on planet earth. We are living in the age that could experience the coming of the Lord. Have you really stopped and thought about that fact? Is there anything more important than the return of Jesus Christ? I can tell you the answer is a resounding *"no"*! And the fact of the matter is that we all must make a personal choice about who we believe Jesus is.

I would like to take this opportunity to make a very important point. We hear and use the words "Jesus Christ" together in our everyday language and we see those two words together in the Bible and in the process, we've lost the meaning of those words.

His name is "Jesus". But listen..."Christ" is *not* His last name... Let me repeat that..."Christ" is not His last name... Please grasp this; "Christ" is His title, not His name. We should actually say that He is "Jesus THE Christ".

The word "Christ" in the Greek language is the word *christos* and this word means "The Anointed One", "The Messiah", "The One chosen by God to bring liberty from sin and peace with God", "The one who will come again to bring all things under God's control". These are all part of the definition of the word *christos*.

Jesus is the "Messiah"; Jesus is the "Anointed One"; Jesus is the "One chosen by God to bring liberty from sin and peace with God"; Jesus is the "One who will come again to bring all things under God's control".

"Everyone who believes that Jesus is the Christ is born of God" (1 John 5:1).

When Jesus asked the disciples who they said He was, Peter responded...

"You are the Christ, the Son of the living God" (Matthew 16:16).

Do you see that small but very important point? Jesus is *the* Christ. And when I came to this pro-found understanding of who Jesus is that He is *the* Christ... it changed me and it showed me another reason why...

There is no turning back...

At this point in my life, I knew that the LORD's hand was upon me and that He was beginning to prepare me for the rest of my life here on earth... and while I had no idea what He would do with me in the future, I knew that He owned me and He could do whatever He wanted to do with my life from here on. My part is to seek Him and His Kingdom...

"Seek first the Kingdom of God and His righteousness, and all these things shall be added to you" (Matthew 6:33).

Our first priority is to seek Him, then...

> *"He will do exceedingly, abundantly above all that we ask or think, according to the power that works in us, to Him be the glory in the church by Christ Jesus"* *(Ephesians 3:20, 21).*

I knew then... and I know now...

There is no turning back!

Chapter 11

Obedience

—〰—

When talking about "prosperity", you may be surprised to see "obedience" in this section.

Somehow, somewhere along the way, the words "obedience" and "holiness" seem to have gotten a bad image. People tend to associate these two words with "works" and want to point out that we are saved by grace, not by "works". I couldn't agree more that we are saved by grace and thanks be to God for that because if any of us were to be saved by "works", then none of us would make it, especially me. But the fact that we ARE saved by grace should cause us to want to do good "works", not to earn our salvation, but because of the gift of salvation in Christ Jesus.

> *For by grace you have been saved through faith, and that not of yourselves; it is the gift of God, not of works, lest anyone should boast. For we are His workmanship, created in Christ Jesus for good works, which God prepared beforehand that we should walk in them. (Ephesians 2:8-10)*

171

Most people know the first part of this Scripture about "by grace you have been saved... not of works, lest anyone should boast," but tend to forget the last part about "good works... that we should walk in them". For us to walk in good works, obedience to the word of God should be a priority in our lives.

Obedience Brings Freedom

In my opinion, obedience to the word of God is where the real freedom is. What most people don't realize is that we are all slaves to either sin or slaves to righteousness. This may not be a popular image, but the word of God is clear...

> *Do you not know that to whom you present yourselves slaves to obey, you are that one's slaves whom you obey, whether of sin leading to death, or of obedience leading to righteousness? But God be thanked that though you were slaves of sin, yet you obeyed from the heart that form of doctrine to which you were delivered. And having been set free from sin, you became slaves of righteousness. I speak in human terms because of the weakness of your flesh. For just as you presented your members as slaves of uncleanness, and of lawlessness leading to more lawlessness, so now present your members as slaves of righteousness, for holiness. Romans 6:16-19*

Now... first let me clear up the word "slave". The Greek word is *doulos* and it means "servant", but a servant "under control of". Jesus used the same word when He said...

> *"A servant is not greater than His master"*
> *(John 15:20).*

These verses in Romans give us a picture that before being born again, we have been under the control of sin. Most people think that when they become a Christian, the fun and freedom ends. Nothing could be farther from the truth. The lie is that we're free to do what we want until we become a Christian, but what most fail to grasp is: *that* life ultimately leads to spiritual death.

The true freedom is a life surrendered to Jesus as Lord, where the guilt, the shame and the lies all end. And in *that* freedom there is real peace.

Please understand two things here: First; I am not perfect, nor will I be this side of Heaven, but now there is forgiveness when I stumble. I am cleansed in the blood of Jesus and I am free from having to try and perform to be good enough. I will never be good enough, but that's the point, I don't have to be good enough. Jesus was good enough. Now I can rest in His freedom that He provides for me.

Second, we MUST understand that a life of obedience is not possible without the help of the Holy Spirit. The Holy Spirit is our guide, our strength, our compass. He empowers us to live a life of obedience that is not possible without Him. Without His help, we rely on our own strength... and a life of obedience is a life of continual failure. However, because of the freedom that Christ provides and with the Holy Spirit leading our life, everything changes for us.

Now, things that used to mean something to me no longer do. And things that I once couldn't imagine are now important to me. My priorities have changed into the priorities that He wants for me and He leads me in paths of righteousness for His name's sake.

And the great news is that these things lead to spiritual life instead of death and into a life of holiness. For example: I used to laugh at obscene stories, I used to use profanity, I used to enjoy going to clubs and sports bars all the time and I would watch all the sports that I could. I used to love the things of the world, but now the Lord has changed me. I don't swear anymore, when the obscene stories start I leave the room if possible, I have no desire to go to the bars anymore and most of the things of the world disgust me. And this is huge: I don't watch very much in the way of sports anymore. Not that sports are wrong, but with many people sports become idolatry. Simply put, the Lord has changed my priorities to His priorities.

Obedience is an Honor

Let's look at a few examples of what the LORD says about obedience. And as we do this, try not to think of obedience as a "work", but an "honor".

The first instance is in 1 Samuel. Here's the setting: The people of Israel wanted a king and so the prophet Samuel begins by anointing Saul king over the nation...

> *"Samuel said to Saul, 'The LORD sent*
> *me to anoint you king over His people,*
> *over Israel. Now therefore, heed the voice*

*of the words of the LORD. Thus says the
LORD of hosts...'" (1 Samuel 15:1, 2).*

Two things jump off the page here: (1) God is
blessing Saul with becoming king of Israel! (2) God
says..."Heed the voice of the words of the LORD."
Translation: "Do what I say here... I have just made
you king over Israel."

Next: The LORD tells Saul to go attack the
Amalekites and destroy everything, but to take
nothing... but Saul decides to keep some of the
spoils of the victory, directly violating what God had
told him to do. In verse 10 the Bible reads...

*"Now the word of the LORD came to
Samuel, saying, 'I greatly regret that
I have set up Saul as king, for he has
turned back from following Me and has
not performed My commandments'" (1
Samuel 15:10, 11).*

Saul had decided that it wasn't that important
to obey the word of the LORD. Listen as Samuel
continues...

*"Why then did you not obey the voice of
the LORD? Why did you swoop down on
the spoil, and do evil in the sight of the
LORD?" So Samuel said, "Has the LORD
as great delight in burnt offerings and
sacrifices, as in obeying the voice of the
LORD? Behold, to obey is better than sacrifice, and to heed than the fat of rams.
For rebellion is as the sin of witchcraft,
and stubbornness is as iniquity and*

idolatry, because you have rejected the word of the LORD, He has rejected you from being king." (1 Samuel 15:19, 22, 23)

Please catch this: "to obey is better than sacrifice" ...this tells us how important God thinks it is to obey Him.

And notice also: "rebellion is as the sin of witchcraft and stubbornness is as iniquity and idolatry" ...as bad as witchcraft? God hates witchcraft, so He must also hate disobedience.

I remember when I came across this section of Scripture; I was taken back at how serious the LORD views obedience and how much He detests rebellion.

Obedience Brings the Blessings

Through Isaiah the LORD speaks to the nation of Israel over and over about obedience versus rebellion...

"Come now, and let us reason together," says the LORD... "if you are willing and obedient, you shall eat the good of the land; but if you refuse and rebel, you shall be devoured by the sword, for the mouth of the LORD has spoken." Isaiah 1:19, 20

I like the fact that God says, "let us reason together"...He wants us to *understand* why He expects obedience: because *he wants to bless us!*

He says that if we are "willing and obedient" we will eat *the good of the land.* That word "good" in the Hebrew language means "the very best". In other words, God is saying, "If you are willing and obedient, you will eat the very best of the land." Not just the "good", but the "very best".

Notice one more small, but very important word there in verse 19 – the word "willing". God doesn't want us to just be "obedient", He wants us to be "willing" to be obedient. You may think... "Craig, what's the big deal here...if I'm obedient, that should show that I'm willing"...but God doesn't want us to view obedience as being a bunch of rules and regulations... He wants us to be obedient out of the Spirit. When we desire to live a life of obedience with the help and guidance of the Holy Spirit, that's a whole different life. Then there's joy in obedience, there's peace in obedience and we are blessed by obedience.

Now do you understand what I mean when I say there are blessings tied to obedience?

Psalm 1 is really the foundation for the entire book of Psalms, with a consistent theme throughout the book. Listen to these words from the LORD...

Blessed is the man who walks not in the counsel of the ungodly, nor stands in the path of the sinners, nor sits in the seat of the scornful; but his delight is in the law of the LORD, and in His law he meditates day and night. He shall be like a tree planted by the rivers of water, that brings forth its fruit in its season, and whatever he does shall prosper... For the LORD knows the way of the righteous, but the way of the ungodly shall perish. (Psalm 1:1-3, 6)

I love this Scripture!

Please notice the very first word: *blessed*. There is a blessing associated with *not* running around with the ungodly, or sinners, or the scornful. Then it says there is "delight" in meditating on the word of God. I am a witness to this because I spend my time meditating on the word and it is an honor and a delight. It is important to know that when we see the word "law" in Scripture, it means "precept" or "statute". In other words, it means "instruction" and we should receive it in a positive manner.

Then notice that when things get tough, we will be like a tree planted by the rivers of water. Have you ever looked at trees planted by water? They are the healthiest trees around because they get plenty of moisture and nutrients.

In addition to that, it says that our "leaf will not wither". What that means is that whatever we're doing will not fail.

And then it says that "whatever we do will prosper". The word "prosper" there is *tsalach* and it means "be profitable".

Now I may not be the smartest one in the room, but I get this! It's as if God is saying here: "If you will separate yourself from the things of the world and give yourself to Me and My word, I will bless you, guard you and you will be successful in whatever you do."

How could anyone *not* want to grab ahold of these promises and *do them*?

Let me give you one more Scripture that the Holy Spirit showed me about the blessings of obedience...

This Book of the Law shall not depart from your mouth, but you shall meditate in it day and night, that you may observe to do according to all that is written in it. For then you will make your way prosperous, and then you will have good success. (Joshua 1:8)

Do you see the words: "prosperous", "good", "success"? What part of this would we *not* want? If someone came to us and said, "I will protect you and I will guarantee your future success, if you will just do what I ask you to do." Who would *not* say yes to that?

Allow me to give personal testimony to this. Stop and think about my situation for a moment... Here I am, a man in his mid-forties and I am in prison. I had lost everything at this point. I didn't have a college degree, a wealthy family to rely upon, or money stashed away somewhere. In other words, by the world's standards I had nothing going for me.

But... I no longer live my life by the world's standards... my provider is the LORD God Almighty and when He says He'll bless me if I'm obedient, I believe Him. I walked out of prison on January 2, 2002 and today I am SO blessed. The LORD has opened doors for me all over America as a public speaker and evangelist. He has blessed me with a great marriage to the girl of my dreams. He has given me a wonderful ministry, success in business; He has healed me from years of addiction and He's not done yet.

So I will restore to you the years that the swarming locust has eaten, the crawling locust, the consuming locust, and the chewing locust, My great army which I sent among you. You shall eat in plenty

179

*and be satisfied, and praise the name of
the LORD your God. (Joel 2:25, 26).*

This is what the LORD has done in my life... He
has restored the years that the enemy had stolen.
God is *so* good to those who will trust Him and seek
Him and obey Him. That's why I say it is an "honor"
to obey the LORD.

Jesus Deserves Our Obedience

We hear people say from time to time, "I would
die for you," but the truth is that not many of us
really would die for someone else. I can say that I
would die for Micah and I believe that I would, but
we really don't know until we are put to the test
and most of us won't ever have to take that test.
However, Jesus was put to that test and when He
was, He passed the test.

We see the cross, we may wear the cross, we put
crosses up in our homes, but most of us, including
myself, can't fully wrap our minds around the
experience that Jesus went through on the cross.
There is no way you and I could take a beating like
He took. And crucifixion was well known as the
most painful, humiliating death penalty there was.
In today's world, we would be appalled to hear of
someone being tortured and killed by crucifixion.

Most of us saw the film *Passion of the Christ* and
it was graphic, but it still can't give the real picture
of the pain and suffering that Jesus went through.
One of the aspects that the film can't capture is the
absolute devastation that Jesus felt at the separation between Him and the Father...

"My God, My God, why have You for-saken Me?" (Mark 15:34)

Here's Jesus, the Son of God who knew no sin, taking a beating for me and you that we couldn't take, going to the cross to be crucified for the sins of all mankind and *then* He had to endure separation from God the Father. As difficult as it is for us... we should all pause and meditate about the details of what Jesus suffered for people like you and me. He suffered as no one ever before or no one after has. And then He prayed for the people who were doing this to Him, while they were doing it.

Because of all this, don't you agree? *Jesus deserves our obedience!*

Obedience Because He's Our Lord

Many people claim Jesus as their Savior, but when I ask about Him being their Lord, they get kind of a confused look on their face.

He *is* our Savior: but He is also our Lord.

Let me explain: the word "Lord" used in the New Testament in reference to Jesus is almost always the word *kurios*, which means "Master who is supreme in authority". The word picture is of someone who is in control of another. This means that as Lord of our lives, He should have authority over us and we should willingly submit to that authority.

The devil lies to us and paints a negative image of this as a God who is just waiting for a chance to punish us and nothing could be further from the truth.

I can testify that with Jesus as Lord, my life has that peace to it that I've been talking about that surpasses all understanding. I love the thought of Jesus as Lord of my life because I've already proven that when He wasn't Lord, my life was a train wreck.

Another benefit in having Jesus as Lord is that someone is directing my life that has power, wisdom and insight that I don't have. I don't have all the answers to life's problems, but I don't have to have all the answers, because Jesus does. Try to imagine Jesus actually directing the day to day activities of our lives. From the moment we wake up until we lay our head down on our pillow, Jesus being in control of our life. I love that thought. I think that's what He meant when He said...

> *"Come to Me, all you who labor and are heavy laden, and I will give you rest. Take my yoke upon you and learn from Me, for I am gentle and lowly in heart, and you will find rest for your souls. For My yoke is easy, and My burden is light"* *(Matthew 11:28-30).*

When we allow Jesus to be Lord, we can finally rest in Him. He takes the reigns of our life and we can relax. If you've ever seen two oxen with that wooden piece around their necks, that's called a "yoke" and one leads the other and they work together. That's the picture Jesus gives us here. He will "yoke" together with us and lead us if we will yield to Him as Lord. My... what a sweet picture of Jesus leading us in our daily walk of life.

When Jesus is Lord of my life, He intercedes with the Father on my behalf.

"For there is one God and one Mediator between God and men, the Man Christ Jesus" (1 Timothy 2:5).

To know that Jesus is interceding on our behalf with our Father is difficult for us to grasp, but if we can wrap our minds around that image it should give us tremendous comfort. Even before we mess things up... Jesus is probably talking to the Father on our behalf. If we had any idea the amount of times that He has stepped in for us as our Mediator, we would be overcome with gratitude. I know that I have no idea the times He's probably said to Father God, "Look, it's Craig again, but I want to intercede on his behalf... I paid for his sin here and I want You to put it on My account. Can We forgive him again?" And the Father says... "Of course My Son." Thanks be to God for His mercy towards me and His grace towards me in His Son Christ Jesus, my Lord.

When discussing this concept of Jesus as Lord, I think it's important to hear what He said. When using this word, *kurios*, He said...

"Why do you call Me 'Lord, Lord,' and not do the things which I say?" (Luke 6:46).

Don't you love the simplicity of Jesus's words?

Here I can almost feel Jesus imploring us to trust Him enough to not just give Him lip service, but to surrender to His Lordship in our lives because if we will do that, He will take care of things that we're not equipped to take care of.

Listen as He continues in Luke...

Whoever comes to Me, and hears My sayings and does them, I will show you whom he is like: He is like a man building a house who dug deep and laid foundation on the rock. And when the flood arose, the stream beat vehemently against that house, and could not shake it, for it was founded on the rock. But he who heard and did nothing is like a man who built a house on the earth without a foundation, against which the stream beat vehemently, and immediately it fell. And the ruin of that house was great. (Luke 6:47-49)

Please notice: both men heard Jesus sayings, the difference is that one... "does them" and the other "did nothing"...

Notice also that it says "when the flood came" ...not "if" the flood came. My point here is that there *will* be storms in life. Not "if", but "when". And when these storms in life come, one man's house stood and the other man's house fell. The difference was that one was founded on a solid foundation and the other wasn't and that foundation was on the fact that one "hears and does" and the other "hears and does not do".

These words of Jesus should give us both pause if we "hear and do not do" and encouragement if we "hear and do" what He says to do.

Remember earlier in the book I had a chapter titled: "Time to Make a Choice".. Well, that applies here as well: we all have a choice to surrender to Jesus as Lord and to live a life of obedience that leads to a life of blessing.

I made the decision in my life. As I began to then and continue to now and in the future to live my life in obedience to God's word and in surrender to Jesus as Lord... I am amazed over and over again by His goodness towards me, His grace towards me and how good life can be. This is part of the abundant life that Jesus promised when He said...

"I have come that they may have life, and that they may have it more abundantly" *(John 10:10).*

I was on my way towards a different kind of life than I had ever been able to imagine and I wanted more. This was the beginning of what I refer to as a prosperous life. And today, I can't wait to see what my Heavenly Father has around the next corner in life.

Obedience of a Nation

I have mentioned before that we in America have been the most prosperous, powerful nation in history and that our blessings have come from the fact that we were formed as a Christian nation and supported Israel. And now we are having problems that we don't seem to be able to solve. The simple answer is that many in this nation have turned from the Lord and are no longer obedient to His word. It didn't just happen overnight; this has been a gradual slide of disobedience and rebellion to His word.

Allow me to share with you some more verses from Jeremiah. I have told you that we as a nation are very similar to the nation of Israel during the time of Jeremiah. They had turned from the LORD and He implored them over and over again to return to Him...

> *Hear the words of this covenant, and speak to the men of Judah and to the inhabitants of Jerusalem and say to them, "Thus says the LORD God of Israel: 'Cursed is the man who does not obey the words of this covenant which I commanded your fathers in the day I brought them out of the land of Egypt, from the iron furnace saying, "Obey My voice, and do according to all that I command you; so you shall be My people, and I will be your God... Hear the words of this covenant and do them."*
>
> *For I earnestly exhorted your fathers in the day I brought them up out of the land of Egypt, until this day, rising early and exhorting, saying, "Obey My voice." Yet they did not obey or incline their ear, but everyone followed the dictates of his evil heart; therefore I will bring upon them all the words of this covenant, which I commanded them to do, but which they have not done.'" (Jeremiah 11:2-4; 6-8)*

As God, He wants His children to obey His words. As a nation, He is very clear that He expects obedience and there will blessings upon that nation. But if that nation turns and has a rebellious heart, there will be national consequences.

"Blessed is the nation whose God is the LORD, the people He has chosen as His own inheritance" (Psalm 33:12).

Just as I mentioned that it is sad that people don't understand the blessings that come from a life of obedience, the fact that our nation's leaders don't comprehend the direction we've taken and the consequences for that direction is heartbreaking. As Christians we must be in prayer that our leaders will turn back to the LORD in their decision making.

Will you join me in a prayer?

"Lord, I thank You so much for the gift of Your word. I love Your word. And Father, as I continue in my walk with Jesus, I ask that You will continue to give me a heart towards obedience for Your word and a deeper understanding of Jesus as Lord in my life. Both as a nation and personally, we need Your mercy and Your grace and ask that You continue the good work that You've begun in us and that as a nation You will help us to turn back to You at this time in our nation's history. Please forgive us as we confess that we as a nation have turned from You and we have been rebellious to Your word. Create in America a spirit of humility, a spirit of repentance and a willingness to return to You. Help us to trust You and be obedient to You. In Jesus's name, amen."

Chapter 12

Faith

—∿∿—

As I continue to take you through the journey that the LORD has me on, I must talk about the subject of faith.

The word "faith" gets thrown around all the time, but if we really understand what faith is, we would be more careful how we use the term.

When talking about faith, it's important to first of all define what faith is and then it's important to talk about who or what we put our faith in. We've all heard the phrase "blind faith" and in America today there are many people who have exactly that, "blind faith".

So, let's begin by looking at the Biblical definition of faith...

> *"Now faith is the substance of things hoped for, the evidence of things not seen" (Hebrews 11:1).*

And now let's look at what the dictionary defines faith as...

Webster's defines faith as: "belief and trust in and loyalty to God".

Now: allow me to teach on both of these definitions:

First: in Hebrews 11 it says "the substance of things hoped for"...let me give you a practical example of faith at work in my life.

I was still in prison. It was July 4th, 2001 and I was in the experimental faith based program in TDC (Texas Department of Corrections). A group of us men asked the warden if we could meet somewhere in private on this day to pray together. This is not just something that inmates do. This was very out of the normal and we really didn't expect him to grant us this request. But many of the men in this unit had been seeking the LORD and several of us felt as though we were being led to fast and pray for our freedom. I wasn't scheduled to be released for another 14 months, but I felt as though the LORD was doing something. The warden granted our request, which is pretty amazing in and of itself. So we put out the invitation to all the inmates on the unit that we were calling for a "Freedom Fast". Get it? Fourth of July... Freedom... inmates in prison... so... "Freedom Fast"...

The details were we would all fast for the previous day, July 3rd and continue into July 4th. There would be no food eaten and we wanted everyone to spend extra time in the word of God. When fasting, it is important to feed the spirit as you starve the flesh. Spending that extra time in the word is how we feed our spirit.

We weren't sure how many men would actually participate in the fast... there was talk of 100 or more... however, the actual morning of the 4th ...only a small group of men showed up that had been fasting the previous day. It was a little disappointing... until someone counted the number of men. There were *12*. In the Bible numbers are important and when we counted that *there were 12 of us there*, we immediately thought of the "12 apostles", the "12 tribes of Israel". We all felt humbled by the fact that the number was 12.

As we entered into prayer, we could just feel the Holy Spirits presence. My prayer was that I would be released *by the end of the year*. I don't know why that's what I prayed for... I hadn't pre-planned that date... I just felt as though the Holy Spirit was leading me to pray for that date. I even wrote that prayer request down in a journal that I was writing in at the time. This was one of the most remarkable experiences of prayer that I have ever been a part of. This was definitely praying for "something that I hoped for" as it says in Hebrews 11:1.

I have no idea what ended up happening with the rest of those men that were part of that "Freedom Fast" ...because within just a few days I was unexpectedly moved from that unit. However, I can tell you what happened with my situation. In November, five months after that "Freedom Fast", I received something called a RMS, which stands for "Received Mandatory Supervision", from the State of Texas. The date for my release was January 2, 2002 and I was told the only reason it wasn't January 1st is because that was a holiday. *Glory be to God!*

This was a *huge* moment in my faith walk! Faith is what we need for something that we haven't yet received. I prayed for my early release... and it took faith for me to be able to receive it...

"Hope that is seen is not hope, for why does one still hope for what he sees?" *(Romans 8:24)*

"For we walk by faith, not by sight" *(2 Corinthians 5:7).*

I love the way Paul phrases both of these verses.

While I couldn't yet see my early release, that's what I prayed for and was believing for and hoping for back on July 4th.

God wants His children to have faith. But I believe that He wants us to also have an understanding *about* faith. What I mean by that is: faith is one of the most powerful forces in the universe. So it's vitally important that as believers in Jesus Christ we live a life of faith. The word of God plays such a very important role in our faith...

"Faith comes by hearing and hearing by the word of God" (Romans 10:17).

Over and over again Jesus said, "He who has ears to hear, let him hear."

Matthew 11:15; 13:9; 13:43

Mark 4:9; 4:23

Revelation 2:7; 2:11; 2:17; 2:29; 3:6; 3:13; 3:22

These verses may sound silly to some...of course we have ears to hear; what else would ears be for? But Jesus is telling us to have ears to hear His word and His Spirit...

"If anyone has ears to hear, let him hear." Then He said to them, "Take heed what you hear. With the same measure you use, it will be measured to you; and to you who hear, more will be given. For whoever has, to him more will be given; but whoever does not have, even what he has will be taken away from him." (Mark 4:23-25)

One of the main reasons my faith is so strong today is because of the amount of time that I spend studying the Scriptures. I want to encourage everyone: spend quality time in the word of God and it will build your faith. Ask anybody that has strong faith and they will tell you the same.

I mentioned that God wants His children to have faith. Listen to what the Bible says about this...

"But without faith it is impossible to please Him, for he who comes to God must believe that He is, and that He is a rewarder of those who diligently seek Him" (Hebrews 11:6).

I am still today in awe of God's word. This verse in Hebrews is almost as though God is saying, "Go ahead... I challenge you to have faith in Me." He says here that if we will diligently seek Him, have faith in Him and believe in Him, then He will reward us. I love the boldness of my Father. When we trust in Him and have faith in Him... it brings Him honor and glory. The more faith we have in Him, the more we honor Him.

As we look at this precious subject of faith, at the start of the chapter I wrote that it was important that we talk about who or what we put our faith in... so let's do that now.

Who or what do you put your faith in? That may sound like a stupid question, but I don't think it is. Humor me...

I'm sure that this is going to offend some people, but after watching the 2008 presidential election; I witnessed people putting "blind faith" in a man that almost nobody had heard of a few years before. Let's be really transparent here... Many people voted for President Obama because he was going to be the first black president in our nation's history. It was the trendy thing to do. It seemed like a special time in our nation's history and people got swept up in the hype. I get that, but the President of the United States of America is far too important of a position to give to a person based on hype.

Then in 2012, after we had time to watch and listen to his actions and words, we as a people voted him into office again. Perhaps I'm naive, but when people make statements and then their actions are in direct conflict with those statements, it should send up a huge red flag. Take the time to go back and listen to his own words and promises, then look at his actions... they don't match up folks!

What has happened to the concept of holding politicians accountable for their words? When asked about the fact that he hadn't done things that he said he was going to do... the president of the United States said that he thought that every-body understood that there is a "world of difference between campaigning and actually governing." Really... that's your answer? Some of us would call that lying, Mr. President. I'm not trying to judge the President – the Lord and history will do that – but my point here is that most of the nation put their trust in a man and the consequences to us as a nation will be devastating.

We are never to put our faith in another human being...

> *"Cursed is the man who trusts in man... Blessed is the man who trusts in the LORD, and whose hope is the LORD"* *(Jeremiah 17:5, 6).*

> *"Woe to the rebellious children," says the LORD, "who take counsel, but not of Me, and who devise plans, but not of My Spirit" (Isaiah 30:1).*

I watch as others put their faith in their pastor, or their spouse, or their business, or the economy, or any number of other things. This is called "idolatry" and the LORD hates it.

In the book of Micah, God's word is very clear...

> *Do not trust in a friend; do not put your confidence in a companion; guard the doors of your mouth from her who lies in your bosom. For son dishonors father, daughter rises against her mother, daughter-in-law against her mother-in-law, a man's enemies are his own household. Therefore I will look to the LORD; I will wait for the God of my salvation. My God will hear me. (Micah 7:5-7)*

This may seem extreme; however, we've all seen and heard of people that have turned on someone very close to them and it shocks us, but it shouldn't. I love my wife Micah with everything I have, but she will never come before the Lord Jesus Christ and she will never put me before Him as well. Jesus has to be the *only* Lord in our lives.

> *"Jesus answered and said to them. Have faith in God" (Mark 11:22).*

If there was ever a time when people need faith in God... it's now. With the rise in atheism, the increase in deception that Jesus warned about in the last days, the increased assault on everything Christian, the increase of lawlessness that our society is in the midst of – we must be people of faith. In Psalm 27, David pens these words...

> *"I would have lost heart, unless I had believed that I would see the goodness of the LORD in the land of the living" (Psalm 27:13).*

This is no time to lose heart. As I have mentioned before, this is an amazing time to be alive on planet earth. We may well be the generation that witnesses the coming of the Lord Jesus Christ. God is looking for people of faith in these last days. Our faith in Jesus must be the cornerstone of our lives to be effective for the Kingdom of God. I pray often: "LORD, bless me in my faith, strengthen my faith, enlarge my faith for Your Kingdom purposes. In Jesus's name, amen."

There is tremendous power involved in our faith that I want to touch on here.

Obviously there are many great books about faith and I encourage you to read on this subject, but my intention in this book is to be a witness about the power of God in a person's life when they surrender and put their faith in Christ. Over and over again, when Jesus healed people of different diseases and sicknesses, He said to them..."your faith has made you well."

In Matthew 9 we see two instances that I want look at. First, listen to this amazing instance...

> *Suddenly, a woman who had a flow of blood for twelve years came from behind and touched the hem of His garment. For she said to herself, "If only I may touch His garment, I shall be made well." But Jesus turned around, and when He saw her He said, "Be of good cheer, daughter; your faith has made you well." And the woman was made well from that very hour. (Matthew 9:20-22)*

This woman had been sick for 12 years. The same account of this event is recorded in Mark 4 in more detail and it tells us that this woman had been seen be many doctors, but her illness continued to get worse. How many of us try everything else first and then as a last resort we come to Jesus and cry out? Why not come to Jesus as the first option, knowing that all things are possible with Him?

Notice also the desperation in this woman: "She said to herself, 'If only I could touch His garment, I shall be made well.'" It's as if she finally realized... "I don't need these doctors... I need a touch from the Master healer, Jesus."

When I was in the penitentiary, I remember so clearly when I hit my knees and cried out to the Lord... in desperation..."I need a touch from the Master healer, Jesus!" It's at that place of desperation... that place of brokenness that we realize that He's our only hope. And it's as if He tenderly responds... "I have been here the whole time... and I love you... and yes, I will heal you, because you've come to Me in faith."

Notice finally: Jesus says to her, "Your faith has made you well." Her faith made her well. When she put all of her faith in Jesus, she was made well. And she was made well immediately, from that very hour. When I put all my faith in Jesus, my life changed and it began to change immediately, even in prison.

As Jesus healed this woman, He was on His way to a ruler's home where the man's daughter had died. It says in Mark 9:23-25 that Jesus went into the house and raised the little girl from the dead. This amazing event is mentioned almost in a matter of fact way, but pause and grab ahold of the scene. Jesus heals this lady on the way to raising someone from the dead! We really can't grasp what this must have been like to be a follower of Christ and to witness these events. Then the Bible continues...

When Jesus departed from there, two blind men followed Him, crying out and saying, "Son of David, have mercy on us!" And when He had come into the house, the blind men came to Him. And Jesus said to them, "Do you believe that

*I am able to do this?" They said to Him,
"Yes, Lord." Then He touched their eyes,
saying, "According to your faith let it be
to you." And their eyes were opened.
(Matthew 9:27-30)*

Once again, notice the desperation of these two
men. They were blind, yet they didn't care what
anyone else thought of them, they just wanted to
be healed.

But the part of this story that really jumps off
the page to me is: when Jesus says to them...
"According to your faith let it be to you." Please
don't miss that... it's too important...

So, if Jesus said that to these two guys...could
this also apply to you and me? I say a resounding
"yes" ...let me repeat those words again by Jesus...

"According to your faith let it be to you!"

When I came across this section of Scripture, I
almost had to be peeled off the ceiling. This sentence spoken by Jesus was revolutionary in my
life. If Jesus said these words... and He did... and
He is no respecter of persons... which He's not...
and the word of God is alive and active... which
it is... then these words *do* apply to me... so...
"According to my faith let it be done to me!"

Even now as I sit by a river in Colorado writing
these words... I want to shout praises to my Father
in Heaven. I must stop here and pray something
that the Holy Spirit has put in my spirit to pray...

LORD, I ask in the name of Jesus, according to
my faith that You put 11 million copies or more,
of this book into people's hands that need Your

touch, that need Your encouragement, that need to hear from another brother in Christ that You're real and that what You've done in my life, You *can* and *will* do in anyone's life if they will totally surrender to You. That You are God Almighty, El-Shaddai – the "God of More Than Enough" ...and that You will do "exceedingly abundantly above all that we ask or think, according to the power that works in us, to You be glory in the church by Christ Jesus to all generations, forever and ever. Amen.

The Lord has been laying this on me for a while, to pray specifically for this book and every time before I write, I get still and say to the LORD... "Ok, LORD... You write this... let these words be Your words... I am not a writer...I didn't want to write this book, so You write it... I will be obedient... but please LORD, keep me out of the way and You write what You want to write. Use this book for Your Kingdom purposes. In Jesus's name, amen."

What area in your life are you desperate for a touch from Jesus? What is it that you need to pray and say... "LORD, according to my faith let it be done to me"?

God loves it when we pray for something that only He can do... that stretches our faith in Him.

God uses ordinary people who have the faith to believe Him and He does great things with them and through them. He does the work; our part is to have the *faith in Him.*

In Hebrews 11, starting in verse 4, we read about ordinary people that God did amazing things with. The thing that set these people apart from others was their faith:

"Abel offered to God a more excellent sacrifice than Cain" (11:4).

"By faith Enoch was taken away so that he did not see death, and was not found, because God had taken him; for before he was taken he had a testimony, that he pleased God" (11:5)

"By faith Noah, being divinely warned of things not yet seen, moved with Godly fear, prepared an ark for the saving of his household, by which he condemned the world and became heir of righteousness which is according to faith" (11:7).

"By faith Abraham obeyed when he was called to go out to the place which he would receive as an inheritance. And he went out, not knowing where he was going" (11:8).

"By faith Sarah herself also received strength to conceive seed, and she bore a child when she was past the age, because she judged Him faithful who had promised. Therefore from one man, and him as good as dead, were born as many as the stars of the sky in multitude – innumerable as the sand which is by the seashore" (11:11, 12).

"These all died in faith, not having received the promises, but having seen them afar off were assured of them, embraced them

*and confessed that they were strangers
and pilgrims on the earth" (11:13).*

Then in that same chapter the Bible goes on to
describe Isaac, Jacob, Joseph, Moses, Rahab and
still others... and finally, listen to these verses concerning faith...

*Therefore we also, since we are sur-
rounded by so great a cloud of witnesses,
let us lay aside every weight, and the sin
that so easily ensnares us, and let us run
the race that is set before us, looking unto
Jesus, the author and finisher of our faith,
who for the joy that was set before Him
endured the cross, despising the shame,
and has sat down at the right hand of the
throne of God. (Hebrews 12:1, 2)*

The conclusion: it's about the "author and finisher
of our faith: Jesus"!

This is what faith is *all* about: it's about
Jesus Christ!

By putting our faith in Jesus and Jesus alone, we
are saved.

I want to be a person of faith. *We* must be a people
of faith. The stakes are high (there are souls at stake);
the day is late; Jesus Christ is coming back soon!

*"Nevertheless, when the Son of Man
comes, will He really find faith on the
earth?" (Luke 18:8).*

This is a very sobering question: "Will Jesus really
find faith on the earth?"

Listen to someone who has had one foot in hell and been brought back...

I promise you... *He's coming back!* I've studied the Bible intensely for the last twelve years... and without any hesitation I can tell you... it's true... it can be trusted... what the Bible says is going to happen... is going to happen!

> *For you have need of endurance, so that after you have done the will of God, you may receive the promise: For yet a little while, and He who is coming will come and will not tarry. Now the just shall live by faith; but if anyone draws back, My soul has no pleasure in him. But we are not of those who draw back to perdition, but of those who believe to the saving of the soul. (Hebrews 10:36-39)*

These are not my words, they are the words of the living God Almighty.

As I continue in my walk with the LORD, I want to continue to grow in my faith. And the times when I need help with my faith, I will ask the Lord to strengthen my faith.

What an amazing God we serve. What a privilege it is to be called one of God's kids. And what a gift it is to have our names written in the Lamb's Book of Life.

As the Lord continues His good work in me in the area of my faith... the Holy Spirit has revealed to me that we're never going to be done growing in Christ this side of Heaven... so with that in mind, let's continue on this journey...

Chapter 13

Time to Grow Up

—〰—

As the LORD was taking me through the transformation process, one of the things that really became evident to me was the growth in my spiritual life that was taking place. Here I was, a man in his mid-forties that the LORD was completely remaking. He was literally changing everything about me, from my likes and dislikes to the way I spoke; my viewpoints and values, to any goals that I may have had in life. This was a total transformation that was taking place and the Holy Spirit was completely in charge. As I look back on my time in prison (I know this sounds so odd) I have fond memories because this was a time of tremendous growth for me spiritually.

There were times when I thought to myself: what a blessing. Where else can a man basically say: "Time out. I am going to take a break from life, go into seclusion and examine my life up until this point? And then I am going to allow the LORD to do His work in my life that He wants to do. To be still while He begins the process of transforming my life." From a spiritual standpoint, I felt as though I was transitioning from being a child into manhood.

In some ways I felt like I was in a monastery. The LORD was making the man out of me that I couldn't do on my own.

Paul spoke about this in 1 Corinthians...

> *"When I was a child, I spoke as a child, I understood as a child, I thought as a child; but when I became a man, I put away childish things"* (1 Corinthians 13:11).

The realization that for so many years I had acted childish in my self-centered lifestyle, I had made decisions without thinking of the consequences; I had lived a life of rebellion against my Heavenly Father, I had hurt many people along the road with no regard for their well-being and I had wasted years of my life without a Godly purpose – all these thoughts had a profound effect upon me. So... as Paul said... I knew that it was time to grow up and become the man that God had called me to be.

I would like to make a point here regarding this subject: in the penitentiary, on Mother's Day, everybody sends out cards to their mothers. But on Father's Day, no one – and I mean no one – sends out cards. I was shocked. So I began to really think about this and here is what I have found out. If you ask 100 people, "Who has had the greatest spiritual influence in your life?" most of the time they will tell you: "My mother," or "My grandmother.'" Now, thank God for Godly mothers and grandmothers, but this is *not* who God intended to be the spiritual head in the family.

The Bible consistently teaches that the man is to be the spiritual head of the family. However, in many, many homes today this is not the case. Not in all homes, but in a large majority, the woman is the spiritual leader. The man of the house has not fulfilled his role as the head. This is tragic. I believe this is one of the reasons that we are at the place we're at in this country today.

Again, not all, but for the most part we men have dropped the ball spiritually speaking in this nation. We have not been the Godly husbands, fathers and spiritual heads of our families that we were called to be.

While I didn't yet know what the LORD had planned for my future, I knew that the process He was doing in me was one of tremendous growth and I deeply wanted whatever He had for me. And while I still have a long way to grow, I am not the person that I once was. I want to be the man that the LORD has called me to be; whatever that may be. Listen to how Paul described this...

> *Brethren, I do not count myself to have apprehended; but one thing I do, forgetting those things which are behind, and reaching forward to those things which are ahead, I press toward the goal for the prize of the upward call of God in Christ Jesus. (Philippians 3:13, 14)*

Paul was striving to become the person that God had called him to be. This was a man that understood his purpose. It may have taken him a while, but once Paul knew his purpose in life, he ran the race set before him with all the strength he had. It also says there in Philippians: "the upward call of God in Christ Jesus."

The "upward call" – men and women, do you understand that we have an "upward call"? What exactly does that mean? It means that there is a "call"; the Greek word is *klesis* and it means "invitation". God is offering us an "invitation" to be about His Kingdom business. So... if there is an "invitation" from God for us to join Him in His business, don't you think we should answer that "invitation" and join Him? You may say... "Ok, Craig... I'm in... but what does that mean?"

It means that it's time to get serious about the things of God, such as:

- How's your daily walk? When you stumble, are you convicted by it? And if you are... do you stop, confess your sin and ask the Holy Spirit to help you in that area of weakness? That's called growing in holiness. It's part of the sanctification process.
- How's your prayer life? Ask the Lord to bless you in your prayer life. Then commit to becoming a man or woman of prayer. You can pray anywhere, at any time. You should try to pray for your family daily; pray for your fellow workers; pray for our nation; pray for your sanctification; pray for Israel; pray that Jesus come soon. Are you getting the picture? The Bible says to pray about everything.
- How's your language? Ask the Lord to help you change your language. It might be profanity, or anger, or harsh words towards others, or obscene jokes or just negative words that are contrary to God's words... ask the Holy Spirit to help your words line up with His words...

- Will you tell your wife or husband, child, or someone else close to you that you want to pray with them... and then pray with them?
- Will you speak up about the things of God... call evil what it is, evil... and call good what it is – good? "Woe to those who call evil good and good evil" (Isaiah 5:20).
- Will you become unashamed of the Gospel? "I am not ashamed of the Gospel of Christ" (Romans 1:16).
- Will you ask the Lord to change you in ways that He wants to change you and then let your light shine? "Let your light shine before men, that they may see your good works and glorify your Father in Heaven" (Matthew 5:16).
- Will you be the "salt" that Jesus told you to be? "You are the salt of the earth; but if the salt loses its flavor, how shall it be seasoned? It is then good for nothing but to be thrown out and trampled underfoot by men" (Matthew 5:13).
- These are all ways that we answer the "invitation" to the "upward call in Christ Jesus."

I am a student of Paul; here was a man that was raised a strict Jew, he had a religious spirit, but he was an enemy of Jesus Christ. He had tremendous zeal in life, even if it was misdirected. But once Paul was made aware of his purpose, he was a warrior for Christ. In that same chapter in Philippians, he talks about this...

Yet indeed I also count all things loss for the excellence of the knowledge of Christ Jesus my Lord, for whom I have suffered the loss of all things, and count them as rubbish, that I may gain Christ and be found in Him, not having my own righteousness, which is from the law, but that which is through faith in Christ, the righteousness which is from God by faith; that I may know Him and the power of His resurrection, and the fellowship of His sufferings, being conformed to His death, if, by any means, I may attain to the resurrection from the dead. Not that I have already attained or am already perfected; but I press on, that I may lay hold of that for which Christ Jesus has also laid hold of me. (Philippians 3:8-12)

Here we can feel the urgency in Paul; he wanted to continue to grow in Christ and be what God called him to be and I want that as well in my life. We should all want to grow in Christ and in the knowledge of Him and His word.

From Milk to Solid Food

This brings me to my next point about growing in Christ. How are we to grow spiritually? The answer is very simple, yet profound and surprisingly, there are many who are not growing because of this area of neglect...

"Therefore, laying aside all malice, all deceit, hypocrisy, envy, and all evil speaking, as newborn babes, desire the pure milk of the word, that you may grow

thereby, if indeed you have tasted that the Lord is gracious" (1 Peter 2:1-3).

Notice the phrase "as newborn babes, desire the pure milk of the word, that you may grow". This is such a beautiful word picture of our growth as Christians. The word of God is our spiritual food. That's how we grow. If you don't feed a child, that child won't grow up to be strong and healthy. I asked my daughter, who is a neonatal nurse, about this and she told me that if a child is malnourished, there will most likely be "stunted development" of that child. That's the term she used, "stunted development" and I think that's a great picture of what happens to those who don't feed on the word of God. We have "stunted development" spiritually speaking.

I see so many Christians that go to church on Sunday; they listen to the pastor's message, then they come home and don't open their Bibles again until the next Sunday. Or they may even go to a Bible study during the week, but again, go home and not open their Bible again until Sunday.

Please take this counsel in a loving manner: that's simply not enough! We need to feed our spirit daily, just like we feed our bodies earthly food daily. Would you only eat twice a week and say, "I'm just too busy"? Of course not, but we do exactly that to our spirit. We, as individuals and in a large part as a nation, are starving spiritually.

I frequently get calls from Christian parents who say that they have raised their kids in the church and recently their kids have come under spiritual attack. Many of these kids are teenagers. They tell me that they feel as though they are losing their kid and that they don't know what to do. And then they tell me that when their kids have questions about the Bible, they don't know how to answer. That's tragic and that's what I mean when I say we are starving spiritually. We should have answers for our children and we should have answers when others, especially non-believers, have questions about our faith and about the Bible. I'm not saying that we should all be Bible scholars, but we should...

"Always be ready to give a defense to everyone who asks you a reason for the hope that is in you" (1 Peter 3:15).

And if someone asks you a question that you don't have the answer, tell them that you will find out and get back to them. Then go, search the word and get back to them with the answer. This is a great open door for fellowship and witnessing.

This is a major reason why we should study the Scriptures so when an opportunity arises, we are able to be a witness for Christ and His word.

There is another very important reason for us to feed on the word of God...

In the world we live in today, we must be able to discern between good and evil. Where do we go for Godly counsel concerning things that we read or hear? How are we to know if what we hear and read is the truth or a lie? Are we to rely upon a talk show host? Or the media? Or someone at the workplace? Listen to these words...

For though by this time you ought to be teachers, you need someone to teach you again the first principles of the oracles of God; and you have come to need milk and not solid food. For everyone who partakes only of milk is unskilled in the word of righteousness, for he is a babe. But solid food belongs to those who are of full age, that is, those who by reason of use have their senses exercised to discern between good and evil. (Hebrews 5:12-14)

Here again, there is reference to the word of God as food. And there is a distinction between those who feed on milk versus solid food. And please take notice that these verses say that by partaking in the solid food, we are able to discern between good and evil. Here's how this works: we hear or read something that may not quite sound right. We go to the word of God and see what it says about that topic. If it doesn't line up with God's word, we should have a check in our spirit. God will never contradict His word.

With all due respect, I don't care what the world says is right. I don't care what some celebrity's opinion is... *I want to know what the word of God says!* When are we going to wake up to the fact that we live in a fallen world that is lost? How am I to be the spiritual head of my family if I don't know what the word of God says concerning the things in the world?

We've all heard the phrase, "The road to hell is paved with good intentions." That statement is more true than most people realize... Jesus said...

"Enter by the narrow gate; for wide is the gate and broad is the way that leads

to destruction, and there are many who go in by it. How narrow is the gate and difficult is the way which leads to life, and there are few who find it" (Matthew 7:13, 14).

This statement by Jesus is in direct conflict with what the world says... The world says "there are many ways to get to heaven... ultimately we all end up at the same place... different faiths are basically the same... most people are basically good, so they will go to heaven... as long as I try to do my best, I'll make it to heaven... a loving God would never send anyone to hell... I was raised in the church, so I'll go to heaven... I was raised in a good family, so I'll go to heaven..." These are all lies from the enemy of your soul. This is why we *must* study the Scriptures. God's word is clear...

- "There is none righteous, no, not one" (Romans 3:10).
- "All have sinned and fall short of the glory of God" (Romans 3:23).
- "The Lord is long-suffering toward us, not willing that any should perish but that all should come to repentance" (2 Peter 3:9).
- Jesus said... "I am the way, the truth, and the life. No one comes to the Father except through Me" (John 14:6).
- "Nor is there salvation in any other, for there is no other name under heaven given among men by which we must be saved" (Acts 4:12).

We have to spend time in the word to know the word. And we have to know the word to be able to discern between good and evil. And we have to be able to discern between good and evil in the world that we live in today. The enemy comes to steal, kill and destroy. We are in a spiritual battle for our families, our churches and our nation. We have to be people of faith and students of the word of God.

Something else Jesus said in those verses in Matthew is... many are on the road to destruction. That goes against everything that most people think. Most people will say, "Oh, I'm going to heaven", but that's simply not what Jesus says.

Jesus said that in the last days, the spirit of deception would increase and many would be deceived and we are definitely experiencing that deception in these days. As we continue to grow in Christ, we should be able to discern this deception. In addition, we should also become more sensitive to evil...

> *"Abhor what is evil. Cling to what is good" (Romans 12:9).*

In my own growth, the Holy Spirit continues to sensitize me to evil and I literally detest so many things of the world. That word "abhor" means "to detest". As followers of Christ, we will continue to notice the increase in deception, the increase in lawlessness, the increase in evil and it should become more and more apparent to us that we are not citizens of this world, but that our citizenship is in Heaven...

> *"For our citizenship is in Heaven, from which we also eagerly wait for the Savior, the Lord Jesus Christ" (Philippians 3:20).*

Things that used to be important to me are now meaningless and the things of God are the most important things in my life now. This is all part of the growth process; the fact that He changes us to the point that our desires are His desires. That brings me to the next point...

Our spiritual growth comes from the word of God and the work of the Holy Spirit in our lives. We can have mentors that help us and teachers that instruct us, but the growth comes from God...

> *"I planted, Apollos watered, but God gave the increase. So then neither he who plants is anything, nor he who waters, but God who gives the increase"* (1 Corinthians 3:6, 7).

Paul explains here that God is the author of all true spiritual growth. Our part is to come with an open heart to the word and then the Holy Spirit will teach us the things of God and as a result we grow. I remember how excited I was when I came across a Scripture in Jeremiah that gives a picture of this...

> *"Your words were found, and I ate them, and Your word was to me the joy and rejoicing of my heart; for I am called by Your name"* (Jeremiah 15:15, 16).

I still get excited when I meditate on these words. God's word is my spiritual food. And I absolutely love the word of God. The word will cleanse us, the word will transform us, the word will encourage us and the word will instruct us in how to live our lives.

"Can the papyrus grow up without a marsh? Can the reeds flourish without water?" (Job 8:11).

Can a Christian grow without the word of God as food and the Holy Spirit as water? The answer is, "Absolutely not!"

I cannot overstate the importance that the word of God has had and continues to have in my life. The word of God is the plumb line in my life for testing the things I hear, see, experience and read. If something doesn't line up with God's word, then there's a problem. This may sound radical to many and it is radical. But we live in dangerous times and there is so much deception in the world.

Let me share another Scripture about our spiritual growth...

"We should no longer be children, tossed to and fro and carried about with every wind of doctrine, by the trickery of men, in the cunning craftiness of deceitful plotting, but, speaking the truth in love, may grow up in all things into Him who is the head – Christ." (Ephesians 4:14, 15)

As we grow spiritually, we should not be tossed to and fro with various teachings. The Bible tells us in 1 John that we should "not believe every spirit, but test the spirits, whether they are of God; because many false profits have gone out into the world."

This is a real test of our growth in Christ, that we should have discernment that comes from the Holy Spirit to know between what's truth and what's a lie.

Finally, our growth process will not end this side of Heaven. Whether we're 25 or 85, we should still be growing in Christ. And as we continue to grow spiritually, the LORD expects us to not only discern between good and evil, but He expects us to speak up about it. We are called to defend the gospel of Jesus Christ and that takes courage on our part. And that's what we'll look at next...

Chapter 14

Christian Courage

—⟪⟫—

G rowing up in the United States of America, if someone would have ever told me that it would take courage to be a Christian, I would of thought that they were kind of weird. What do you mean? America is a Christian nation; just about everyone in America is a Christian, aren't they? So... why would it take courage to be a Christian?

In this chapter we will take a sobering look at the state of America and the sad fact that today in America, I believe it does take courage to be a Christian. I also want to talk about what a Christian is and isn't.

Where Are The Watchmen?

First: let's talk about this country of ours. I grew up in the 60s, 70s and 80s and when I was growing up I never thought I would see the things that I'm witnessing today. In the America that I grew up in, it was just a forgone conclusion that we were a Christian nation. We were the most blessed country in the world; we knew that we were the most blessed country in the world and we knew that our blessings came from the LORD. I grew up in the south, the Bible Belt, in a suburb of Dallas. Just look around and you'll see a church on almost every corner. Of course we're a Christian nation, right?

The problem is that no one told us that we needed to be on the lookout for an enemy. I will tell you how naive I was – I assumed that most other people around the world were also Christian. If we had an enemy, it was Russia and we knew they were the enemy. I think most of us had no idea that there was a spiritual enemy out there. Most of us never dreamed there was an enemy at work against the soul of our nation. And that this enemy wasn't another country, but an enemy that is more evil than any of us could imagine.

This is a different kind of enemy. The enemy that I'm talking about is patient; this enemy is subtle; this enemy is deceptive; this enemy never sleeps; this enemy isn't visible like the kind of enemy that we're used to fighting against. This enemy comes to steal, kill and destroy. This enemy has a plan and he's smarter than any enemy the United States of America has ever confronted.

In the Old Testament, God said this to Ezekiel...

> *"Son of man, I have made you a watchman for the house of Israel; therefore hear a word from My mouth, and give them a warning from Me" (Ezekiel 3:17).*

I want to give you a picture of what a watchman was. At the time Ezekiel was written, most towns or villages had a wall around them for protection. There was someone appointed as the watchman and this person's duty was to sit on top of the wall and keep watch for enemies. They would look far off into the distance and watch for any approaching enemy forces and then they would warn the people. They would blow a large trumpet that would warn the people that there was an enemy approaching. Thank God for watchmen, because without them a town could be attacked and an enemy could actually enter the camp under the cover of night, without the people ever knowing. The word here in this verse for "watchman" in the Hebrew language is *tsaphah* and it means "to lean forward and peer into the distance" or "to observe and wait". So think about this meaning: a watchman leans forward, looks out into the distance, observes and waits for an enemy, then when he sees the enemy, he blows the trumpet and warns the people. Got the picture?

Now, allow me to apply this to our nation in a spiritual manner. This is very important, because I believe with all my heart that the application of this picture has everything to do with the state of America today. I recently heard a very well-known pastor in America talk about the fact that in the 60s and 70s, when preachers began to water down their messages and began to become more concerned about not offending their congregations than boldly proclaiming the word of God, that is the time that he pinpoints as a turning point in our nation. I couldn't agree more. A pastor's responsibility is not to worry about hurting somebody's feelings. The pastor's responsibility is to rightly divide the word of God and to preach that word. If Jesus were in most of our churches today and spoke the way that he spoke when He was here, He would be asked to leave.

Where Are The Watchmen?

Here's my point: in that verse of Ezekiel God says, "hear a word from My mouth, and give them a warning from Me." So...where are the watchmen? My ministry has a watchman calling on it and I can tell you that it's not real popular to be a watchman. But, watchmen are needed to warn the people about the enemy. And without watchmen, the enemy can ride into camp and begin to attack and he may even be able to attack without being noticed, because there are no watchmen to blow the warning trumpet.

The enemy is Satan. He is patient and many years ago we as a nation began to drift from the LORD. It didn't happen overnight; it couldn't have because there were too many solid Christians in America. Satan knew that he would have to be patient and subtle in his plan to destroy this nation. So slowly he used the spirit of pride and the spirit of complacency to get us to drift from God. We are a proud nation and that pride does not come from the LORD. A humble spirit is from the LORD and for so long our ancestors were humble, hardworking people. But in the 60s and 70s we began to get comfortable and our pride as a nation exploded into a very self-centered, prideful attitude. We knew that we were a great country, but we began to believe it was because of our own greatness and we forgot that it was because of God's hand of blessing and protection. And as we began to drift as a nation...

Where Were The Watchmen?

Then Satan used the sexual revolution in our nation to lead us down a very dangerous path. As a student of God's word, I can assure you that sexual immorality is a very serious subject to the LORD. God destroyed Sodom and Gomorrah for their sexual perversion and the New Testament says...

"Sodom and Gomorrah, and the cities around them in a similar manner to these, having given themselves over to sexual immorality and gone after strange flesh, are set forth as an example, suffering the vengeance of eternal fire" (Jude 8).

When God's word says... "these are set forth as an example," we should have a heightened sensitivity to that. But, we as a nation have *not* heeded this Scripture; we have not listened to God's warning.

Satan first began to desensitize us to the sexual perversion in our nation. Things that we knew were wrong, we've come to accept. Let me give you an example: when I was growing up, in the afternoon on television were shows like The Munsters, Dick Van Dyke, Andy Griffith, Batman... now you'll see reality shows with homosexuals, transvestites, actual physical violence between people and just about anything else that can be imagined. And these shows are on in the middle of the afternoon when small children are at home. And as a result, we now celebrate homosexuality as a lifestyle: something that God calls an abomination!

Isaiah gives a strong warning that we should think about...

"Woe to those who call evil good, and good evil; who put darkness for light, and light for darkness" (Isaiah 5:20).

221

The homosexual movement is one of the areas that we now call good, but God calls evil. No matter how many people disagree with this statement, the Bible is clear on this subject. Homosexuality is sin and God hates sin. There is no other way to say it. God loves the homosexual, but He hates the sin in homosexuals just as He hates the sin in me or anyone else. Folks, we have a problem called sin and God cannot tolerate sin. Sin must be dealt with and thanks be to God that He sent His Son Jesus into the world to deal with the sin that you and I can't. We are to confess our sin; turn from our sin and surrender our lives to Jesus.

Then there's pornography, which has exploded into a multi-billion dollar industry. Tragically, pornography has infiltrated the church. Statistics tell us that as many as 25% of pastors struggle in the area of pornography. As a men's pastor, I can tell you that this problem in the church is much worse than most people realize and to a large extent is being ignored instead of being dealt with. We are supposed to be different from the world and when we're not, it does tremendous damage to our witness. How can we be salt and light in a dark world if we're engulfed in sexual immorality? Take the time to read Romans 1 and hear what God has to say about sexual immorality...

God gave them up to vile passions. For even their women exchanged the natural use for what is against nature. Likewise also the men, leaving the natural use of the woman, burned in their lust for one another, men with men committing what is shameful and receiving in themselves the penalty of their error which was due.

And even as they did not like to retain God in their knowledge, God gave them over to a debased mind, to do those things which are not fitting; being filled with all unrighteousness, sexual morality, wickedness, covetousness, maliciousness; full of envy, murder, strife, deceit, evil-mindedness; they are whisperers, backbiters, haters of God, violent, proud, boasters, inventors of evil things, disobedient to parents, undiscerning, untrustworthy, unloving, unforgiving, unmerciful; who, knowing the righteous judgment of God, that those who practice such things are deserving of death, not only do the same, but also approve of those who practice them. (Romans 1:26-32)

These are very serious verses that we must heed. The church must confront sexual immorality, and ask the Holy Spirit to help us to confess and repent and be an example to the unbelieving world...

It's time to wake up people! And yet...

Where Are The Watchmen?

Almost daily we hear of new violence in our nation. This violence in our nation is at an all-time high. There are entire sections of cities in America that the police will no longer enter into. These areas are like war zones that the police have given up on. This is happening in America! The level of lawlessness has exploded. Jesus talked about this as one of the signs of the last days...

> *"And because lawlessness will abound, the love of many will grow cold"* *(Matthew 24:12).*

Kids killing kids, family members turning against one another and the de-valuing of human life is astounding. With the depravity in our nation today, we will only see an increase in lawlessness as we continue in the last days. When something like what happened in Colorado when the Batman movie was coming out takes place, we all seem to be shocked... but why should we be shocked? These things are a manifestation of our society. It seems as though all restraint is gone in our society today...

> *"Where there is no revelation, the people cast off restraint" (Proverbs 29:18).*

What are we doing as a nation? As we continue to slide down this slope we're on, things will continue to get worse. I am sorry to be the bearer of bad news, but God's word is clear... when a nation turns from Him and His word, there will be consequences. Why can't we understand what is happening to America... why can't we stop right now, confess our sin, repent and turn back to the LORD in humility? Instead, we just continue to go through our daily lives, we allow our leaders to take us in the wrong direction, we listen to celebrities and talk show hosts and then we stand back and shake our heads at the violence and act as though we're shocked that these things are happening. And yet...

Where Are The Watchmen?

Growing up in Dallas in the 70s, I was raised to believe that politicians and government officials were supposed to be the cream of the crop in morality. That sounds like a joke today. What has happened to integrity in government? At every level: city government, school districts, state government and at the national level of government – corruption is rampant. Our government leaders lie, steal, take bribes, cheat the taxpayers and they seem to think they are above the law. Where's the accountability? Not just in politics, but also in business. I know that someone would say that corruption has always been part of business, but that doesn't justify it. When I see the corruption on Wall Street, the mortgage industry, the banking Industry and the overall mindset in business of "I'm going to get mine and I'll do whatever it takes", it really grieves me. How is it that we as a nation think we can conduct our affairs like this without the judgment of God coming upon us? Satan has deceived people into thinking that this is just the way things are done. He has blinded people to the fact that there are consequences for an individual's decisions and there are consequences for a nation's decisions. There is a spirit of arrogance that is prevalent in our society. And yet...

Where Are The Watchmen?

This may sound old fashioned to some people, but my father taught me that a man's word should mean something... He would say, "If a man's word is no good, then he's no good." Jesus had a similar thing to say concerning our words...

*"But let your 'yes' be 'yes' and your 'no',
'no'. For whatever is more than these is
from the evil one" (Matthew 5:37).*

In today's world, a person's word doesn't seem to mean anything. When our own president thinks it's ok to lie, it should cause us to pause and be concerned.

Now, I am not perfect, but I want to live my life in a way that my word means something. I want my "yes" to mean "yes" and my "no" to mean "no". I want to live my life with integrity and I want to be trustworthy in all areas of my life. The Bible teaches that we will be accountable for our words. That's a sobering thought to me, knowing that one day I will stand before God and have to give account for my words. And yet...

Where Are The Watchmen?

The devil has taken us down this path to the place where I no longer recognize the America that I grew up in. We've now taken God out of schools and public places, we've allowed a few to raise their voices so that we've now become intimidated to pray in public, we have rebelled against God's word and don't seem to really care, we began killing babies to the number of over 50 million children and called it "right to choose"; the sexual perversion is to the point where we call the Bible hate speech when it teaches that homosexuality is wrong. God's word not only says it's wrong, He calls it an abomination. That means that He detests it in the strongest of terms.

Let me state something as clearly as I can:

God is God and He doesn't need my approval or yours. When God says something is wrong, it's wrong. It doesn't matter what we, as a nation, want to justify or call right and wrong. There is only *one* final authority and it is God Almighty. And when He says something is wrong, that makes it wrong. Over and over again the Bible states that He is God and He does not change...

> *"For I am the LORD, I do not change"*
> *(Malachi 3:6).*

> *"'You have gone away from My ordi-*
> *nances and have not kept them. Return*
> *to Me, and I will return to you.' says the*
> *LORD of hosts" (Malachi 3:7).*

Do you want New Testament?

> *"Jesus Christ is the same yesterday,*
> *today, and forever. Do not be carried*
> *away with various and strange doc-*
> *trines" (Hebrews 13:8, 9).*

You may call it hate speech, I call it the word of God. You may call it intolerance, I call it instruction in right living. You may call it narrow-minded; I call it obedience. Please listen to these words...

> *"There is a way that seems right to a*
> *man; but its end is the way of death"*
> *(Proverbs 14:12).*

If you have a problem with my viewpoint, that's ok. You'll have an opportunity one day to stand before God Almighty and tell Him that you have a problem with His viewpoint. Please hear this warning: that conversation won't go in your favor. You'll quickly come to the realization that your opinion was wrong, dead wrong. You'll also quickly come to the realization that there is only *one* God in that conversation and it's not you. So I ask again...

Where Are The Watchmen?

This may sound intolerant, but I have to speak out. If you've read this book to this point, you know that I was as lost as anyone can be. You know that God took me and out of His love for me, He had me arrested, put in prison, broke me there and began the transformation process of renewing my mind. He has made me into His witness. And as a witness I have to tell the truth, the whole truth and nothing but the truth, so help me God. And the truth is: we as a nation are in deep trouble. There are still many people that believe God, believe the Bible and if you are one of those people, then you know I am speaking the truth. But for a large percentage of this nation, we have turned away from the Lord and we have deliberately rebelled against His word.

The fact that statistics tell us as many as 60% of confessing Christians believe there is more than one way to get to heaven reveals how far we've drifted from God's word. If we can't get this point right, how are we to defend our faith in a world that is becoming more and more hostile towards the Bible and towards everything Christian?

Jude wrote about this....

"Beloved, while I was very diligent to write to you concerning our common salvation, I found it necessary to write to

228

you exhorting you to contend earnestly for the faith which was once for all delivered to the saints" (Jude 3).

These words could just as easily apply to us in America right now. Are you ready to "contend earnestly for the faith"? In my opinion... there is no higher calling than defending Jesus Christ and our Christian faith. I will defend, stand up for, give a reason for and be prepared to die for Jesus Christ.

I never thought I'd see the day in America when there would be such an open hostility towards Christian beliefs. I never thought that I'd see the day in America when atheists would be so bold. I never thought I'd see the day in America where religious tolerance would be called for except for Christians!

I never thought I'd see the day in America when the Bible would be rejected. I never thought I'd see the day in America when pastors would be censored in the pulpit, but we are just about there. And I never thought I'd see the day in America when the church that was so strong would become so silent.

This is what I mean when I speak about having courage to be a Christian in America. It would be easy to just sit by and say nothing. And unfortunately, that is exactly what is happening.

Let me ask you a question and before you answer or read further, please pause and think about your response.

What is a Christian?

The first time in the Bible that the term is used is in the book of Acts. A man named Barnabas departed for the area known as Tarsus to look for

Saul, who we know is also the name for the Apostle Paul. In chapter 11 we pick up the account and we read in verse 26...

> *"And when he had found him, he brought him to Antioch. So it was that for a whole year they assembled with the church, and taught a great many people. And the disciples were first called Christians in Antioch" (Acts 11:26).*

I would like to focus on one word in that verse... the word "disciple". In the Greek language it is the word *mathetes* and it means "a learner of", "a student", "a follower of". These people who were called "disciples" were students of Christ, they were followers of Christ; they were learners of Christ.

Now let's discuss what a Christian is and isn't in our world today. This section of the book is probably going to offend some people, but as I mentioned earlier in this chapter, the role of a watchman isn't very popular.

If a Christian is a follower of Christ, then he or she should believe in Jesus, but in addition they should also believe the things He said, the things He taught and be willing to defend them and obey them.

> Jesus Himself said... *"Why do you call Me 'Lord, Lord' and not do the things that I say?" (Luke 6:46).*

So... if a person doesn't *do* the things Jesus said, they're really not a follower of Christ. And if a person doesn't *know* what He said or taught, how can they *follow* what He said or taught? I am shocked at how little most confessing Christians really know of what Jesus taught in the Bible. I mean, how can a person know what He taught unless they become a student of His? And a student, by definition, studies. Yet, most people who call themselves Christian don't study the Bible to learn what He taught.

Without purposely trying to offend anyone, allow me to make a few observations.

- Wearing a cross doesn't make someone a follower of Christ.
- Going to church doesn't make someone a follower of Christ.
- Growing up in America doesn't make someone a follower of Christ.
- Getting a t-shirt, a bumper sticker, singing a song, lighting a candle, celebrating Easter or Christmas or thanking God for a meal – none of these things makes someone a follower of Christ.

Jesus said...

"Not everyone who says to Me, 'Lord, Lord,' shall enter the kingdom of heaven, but he who does the will of My Father in heaven. Many will say to Me in that day, 'Lord, Lord, have we not prophesied in Your name, cast out demons in Your name, and done many wonders in Your name?' And then I will declare to them, 'I never knew you; depart from Me, you who practice lawlessness!'" Matthew 7:21-23

To be a Christian is to come to the place where we confess that we are sinners, then repent of our sins (which means to turn from our sins) and to become a follower, a student, a disciple of Jesus and to desire to know Him. This is a life change. This is realizing that my life is no longer my own. This is comprehending what He has done for us and surrendering our lives to Him. This is putting Him first in our lives: before our family, before our job, before our country, before everybody and everything. This means we will not be "politically correct" if it means going against His word. This means being willing to stand for His word even when it's not popular. It may mean having to lose friends, family or possessions for Him. This means we come to the realization that there are going to be times when we will have to make choices and these choices will not always be easy. This means understanding that the world will end up hating us because He said it would get to that point. This means that there is no compromising when it comes to Jesus. He is now Lord over every area of our lives. His word is final, which means that the Bible is the final word. Are you at this place? Does this describe you as a Christian? Hear these words from Paul...

> *"Examine yourselves as to whether you are in the faith. Test yourselves. You know that Jesus Christ is in you – unless indeed you are disqualified"* (2 Corinthians 13:5).

These are bold words from Paul and yet they need to be heard today in America.

This is what it means to be a Christian. I find myself wanting to say..."Stop calling yourself a Christian if you don't mean it. Stop saying there is more than one way to get to heaven than Jesus if you call yourself a Christian. Stop saying that marriage between one man and one woman is intolerant if you call yourself a Christian. Stop saying that speaking out against homosexuality is hate speech if you call yourself a Christian. If you're not ready to defend the faith, to defend the Bible as the word of God and to acknowledge Jesus as Lord of your life, then just stop calling yourself a Christian." Does this offend you? Well, what about offending Jesus Christ who died for you?

Jesus said in Revelation...

> *"I know your works, that you are neither cold nor hot. I could wish you were cold or hot. So then, because you are lukewarm, and neither cold nor hot, I will vomit you out of My mouth" (Revelation 3:15, 16).*

Awfully strong words spoken here by Jesus, aren't they? And yet... these words need to be heard by everyone who calls themselves a Christian in America. Jesus would rather we either get "hot" or get "cold". There is no 50% with Jesus. There is no 92% with Jesus. You are either for Him or you're not. It's 100% in, or 100% out.

Is this startling to hear? It needs to be. It's time for people in America to wake up. The stakes are high. We're talking about people's souls here. We're talking about the fabric of our nation here. We're talking about good versus evil here. We're talking about Jesus Christ versus Satan here.

When I speak in prison, I tell the inmates that when they give their lives to Christ, that's when the battle really begins. I also tell them that it will take courage to become a Christian, because they will have to walk away from most of the things they have associated with in the past. I would also say the same thing to people out in the world. It takes courage to be a Christian today, even in America. It will require that you walk away from many of the things in your past. It may involve ending some relationships that are wrong. The word "repent" means to turn and go the other direction. We have to be willing to turn from things that are not of God and to seek those things that are of God. While we are saved by grace and not of works, that grace will cause us to change many of the works in our life. There will be people who will ridicule us, who will scoff at us, who will call us crazy and who will hate us. You need to come to grips with these things. If anyone comes to Christ and believes that their life will be the same as before, then they have been deceived. If you surrender your life to Christ, things will be different. But the rewards cannot be accurately described.

Every one of us will die at some point in time unless Jesus comes back first. And everyone will spend eternity in either a place called "hell" or a place called "heaven". Both places are real. The Bible teaches clearly that there is a heaven and there is a hell. Whether you or I agree with that teaching doesn't make it so or not so. If the Bible teaches that, then it is settled for me. Jesus taught that heaven and hell are both real places and that He is the only way to enter into heaven.

It takes courage to be a Christian today and it will only get worse in these last days. So prepare your minds, your spirits and your emotions. While Jesus said that no one knows the day or the hour of His return, He also told us there would be signs of His return...

As someone who prays for discernment, I can tell with certainty that we're in the last days before Christ's return. Now, I don't know if that means two years, four years, ten years or longer. No one knows that, but we are told that we can discern the time. We will discuss this at further length in the last chapter, but when we come to the realization that we're in a spiritual battle for the fabric of our nation and our families, we must have the courage to stand for our faith and be willing to speak up about Jesus. We have to make a choice which side we're on...

"If it seems evil to you to serve the LORD, choose for yourselves this day whom you will serve... but as for me and my house, we will serve the LORD" (Joshua 24:15).

When the Jewish people were about to enter the Promised Land, Moses spoke to the people concerning their enemies and he said to them...

"Be strong and of good courage; do not fear nor be afraid of them, for the LORD your God, He is the One who goes with you. He will never leave you nor forsake you" (Deuteronomy 31:6).

Today... the LORD says the same to us: "Be strong and of good courage." We don't have to fear the enemy. We will need courage, but Jesus will never leave us or forsake us; He has promised us that. He has also said...

"He who is in you is greater than he who is in the world" (1 John 4:4).

I want to encourage everyone reading this... have courage... if you're a Christian, we are on the winning side. We are in a war and things may get tough, but we must be strong and have courage... Jesus is coming soon!

And join me in prayer for the LORD to raise up watchmen to watch for the enemy and to sound the warning...

"LORD, we as a nation are in trouble. Thank you for raising up men and women who will not compromise Your word and who will defend the faith. But Father, we have rebelled against You and we humbly ask for Your mercy, Your grace and ask that You would create in all of us a spirit of repentance. We ask that You would look down from Heaven and create a revival in America. A revival ignited by Your Holy Spirit that would sweep this land; cleanse this land and turn us as a nation back to You. LORD, create in us a hunger for Your word, a Godly humility and a heart of obedience. Father, we ask these things not because of who we are, but because of who You are; according to Your mercies and Your forgiveness and Your longsuffering. Look down upon America and continue to use her as a beacon of light in the darkness. Refine us and change us as only You can. Push back the darkness and shine Your light upon us. And finally LORD, send Your Son Jesus back for us soon. Let Your Kingdom come on earth as it is in Heaven. We ask these things in Jesus's name. Amen."

Chapter 15

A New Prayer Life

—∿—

I believe if there is an area that is more neglected, more misunderstood than almost any area in the Christian life, it would be the subject of prayer.

I want to encourage everyone reading this book in the area of prayer. I find it difficult to put into words the privilege that I believe prayer is.

Please – pause with me and really think about this thing we call "prayer". The thought of being be able to communicate with the Creator of the universe is not only humbling, it's just difficult to wrap our minds around.

Webster defines "prayer" as: "To make a request to or address God in a humble manner with adoration, confession, supplication or thanksgiving."

I actually like that definition, but think about what it says... "to address God" ...umm... "Hello, God? Can I talk with You for a few minutes?" Now, forgive me for my simplistic mind here folks... but, to me, that is perhaps the most amazing thought on the planet. Are you trying to tell me... that I, Craig Nedrow, can address God Almighty? If my understanding is correct... that's exactly what that means.

If you or I had the chance to meet with... say, the Queen of England... or the President of the United States... or Billy Graham... or whomever you deem as the most admired person in the world to you... would it be an honor? Of course it would... well, how about meeting with the God who created the universe, who sits on His throne in heaven, who can change any circumstance on this planet? And yet, the Bible tells us that ordinary people like you and I have the privilege of coming to Him with our concerns, our fears, our hopes and dreams and we can come to Him as our Father!

Does this not absolutely blow anybody else away like it does me? This thought leaves me speechless even now as I write this.

To me... if we would really stop and meditate on this fact, it would revolutionize our lives. Everything changes because our perspective is now changed. Allow me to explain.

First of all:

The Gospel: The Good News

If we've been born again, surrendered our lives to Jesus Christ as Lord, then we've now entered into a new family. My father is no longer the devil, the father of lies. My Father is now God Almighty; Jehovah God; the One and only true God. That is a fact that none of us can really fully wrap our minds around this side of heaven. When I talk to someone about salvation, it's impossible for me to accurately express what transpires when we become born again. There is *no* better news in this world than the gospel. That's why the word "gospel" means "good news".

Imagine someone saying to me, "Craig, you get a do over." In golf it's called a "mulligan" and it means that you get to take a shot again. That's a good word picture of being born again. Listen closely to these words...

> *"If anyone is in Christ, he is a new creation; old things have passed away; behold, all things have become new. Now all things are of God, who has reconciled us to Himself through Jesus Christ" (2 Corinthians 5:17, 18).*

Please look again at those five words... "all things have become new"...really? *All?* Yes... "All". It's almost as though I find myself saying... "Wait a minute, God; You obviously don't understand who we're talking about here. We're talking about me, Craig Nedrow. There's no way You're going to allow 'all things to become new' for me... not for someone like me." And He says..."Yes Craig, even for someone like you."

This is not just "good news" to me... this is "You have got to be kidding me" news. But that's what His word says... and that's exactly why it's the "gospel", the "good news". That's why it's a gift, because I can't earn this... I don't deserve this... what I deserve is a trip to hell. And yet, because of God's goodness, He offers someone like me a new life if I will put my trust in His Son Jesus Christ and not in myself. That's why it says...

> *"The goodness of God leads you to repentance" (Romans 2:4).*

Secondly:

Abba: Father

When we are born again, I mentioned that our Father is now God. The word *abba* is an Aramaic word that is only used three times in the Bible. I would encourage you to read these three verses and ask the Holy Spirit to reveal to you what He wants you to know about them. They are:

- Romans 8:15, 16
- Mark 14:36
- Galatians 4:6, 7

> *"For you did not receive the spirit of bondage again to fear, but you received the Spirit of adoption by whom we cry out, 'Abba, Father.' The Spirit Himself bears witness with our spirit that we are children of God"* *(Romans 8:15, 16).*

At this point I want to address the fact that not everyone reading this book has a great image when the word "father" is mentioned. I feel bad about that, because until the day my dad went to be with the lord, we were very close. If the image you have hearing the word "father" is not a good one, I encourage you to ask the Holy Spirit to minister to you about your heavenly Father. We have a Father in heaven that loves us more than any of us can imagine. Even those of us with great dads can't really grasp the love that Father God has for us.

The word *abba* is an Aramaic word that represents the most intimate, trusting, dependent love that a child can have for a father. The closest word that we have in our English language is the word "Daddy". When we hear a child call their parent "daddy", there is a love, a trust, a dependency to it. We may call our father "dad" or "father", but when we use the term "daddy" it represents an additional intimacy.

Jesus, at His point of greatest need, in the garden when He was praying, said...

> *"Abba, Father, all things are possible for You. Take this cup away from Me; nevertheless, not what I will, but what You will" (Mark 14:36).*

Jesus knew that Father God was His only hope and He called Him "Abba" – "Daddy". And if Jesus called Him "Abba", as humbling as this may seem, we can call Him "Abba" as well.

To me... the thought that God is my heavenly Father, but that He is also my "Daddy" – my "Abba" – is overwhelming. That I'm His little boy and that He loves me that way is too wonderful to put into words.

This word "Abba" is not a word to be just read over without pausing and reflecting upon. Even now as I write this, I am going to pause and meditate upon this amazing word that the Scripture has given us.

With these two points in mind: imagine if our Father in heaven, "Abba", said to us: "Tell Me what's going on with you right now. Tell Me about the areas where you've stumbled and let My grace and My Son's blood wash you and cleanse you. You know that I love you; what can I help you with? Tell me about your fears, your anxieties, your concerns.

I am here to help you in anything that you need. I want you to trust Me that I have your best interest at heart. Do you understand that all things are possible for Me? There is nothing too hard for Me. What situation do you need My help with? Who else do you know that needs My help? Pray to Me for those people. What other concerns do you have? Your country, your family, your job, your health, your future? Pray to Me about all these things. Give Me all your cares... because I care for you. There is nothing too small or to great. Now... will you trust Me? Will you relax and believe Me when I tell you that I will work all these things out? You may not understand how, you may not even agree with how I will work out all these things, but one day you'll be able to understand. I see the end from the beginning; and I can change circumstances and events. All things are working according to My plan. You just need to trust Me. Will you do that?"

"Because you are sons, God has sent forth the Spirit of His Son into your hearts, crying out, 'Abba Father!' Therefore you are no longer a slave but a son, and if a son, then an heir of God through Christ" (Galatians 4:6, 7).

"Behold, I am the LORD, the God of all flesh, is there anything too hard for Me?" (Jeremiah 32:27).

"...casting all your care upon Him, for He cares for you" (1 Peter 5:7).

"I am God, and there is none like Me, declaring the end from the beginning" (Isaiah 46:9, 10)

"Trust in the LORD with all your heart and lean not on your own understanding; In all your ways acknowledge Him, and He shall direct your paths" (Proverbs 3:5, 6).

"Your heavenly Father knows that you need all these things. But seek first the Kingdom of God and His righteousness, and all these things shall be added to you" (Matthew 6:32, 33).

"If God is for us, who can be against us?" Romans 8:31

Please notice these verses: they give a wonderful glimpse into the heart of our Father in heaven.

Isn't it awesome to know that we have a Father whom we can call "Abba", "Daddy", that not only loves us, cares about us and is for us, but also has the power to change circumstances in our lives, has the ability and the means to take care of us and has our best interests in mind?

Now that we've laid a foundation here, let me make a few points. And I'll begin with a simple question:

Do You Pray?

Of course I pray, Craig... Really? Because... I ask people "if" they pray and I am shocked at some of the answers that I get. First of all, don't just take for granted that everyone *does* pray...

A friend of mine's wife was recently taking a college class about "religion" and she called and asked me if she could interview me for a class assignment. During this interview the subject of prayer was mentioned and I asked her about her prayer life. She looked at me, thought for a few seconds and said... "I don't think that I've ever prayed before." You could have knocked me off my chair. I stopped and thought... "She can't be serious," but then the realization hit me that not only was she serious, but that she's probably closer to the majority than the minority. Here she was... a mother of two and a wife and she was telling me, in a very matter of fact way, that she had *never* prayed. It almost brought me to tears. I have thought about this quite a bit since we met and I've come to a stark realization...

If there are 300 million or so people in America; and if the numbers are correct; statistics tell us that there are about 75% "Christians" in America. Now... no offense, but I seriously doubt that percentage is correct. But, let's say there are 150 million Christians, or 50% of the American population that are Christians. The numbers vary greatly, but recent polls show that about 40% of those people asked say they seldom if ever pray. If these numbers are even close to correct, that means around 60 million Christians seldom, if ever, pray. I can't speak for anyone else, but I find that fact very disturbing.

And then, in the body of Christ, how many people simply either pray at a meal... or pray at Thanksgiving or Christmas? Or pray as a last resort when they've tried everything else and finally say... "Maybe we should pray." Listen to these words from our Lord Jesus...

"And when you pray..." Matthew 6:5

"But you, when you pray..." Matthew 6:6

"And when you pray..." Matthew 6:7

"In this manner, therefore, pray..."
Matthew 6:9

Please notice that Jesus didn't say..."*if* you pray."
He said "*when*" you pray.

We are told *to pray!* How in this chaotic world
are people getting along without the benefit of
prayer? No wonder so many people are depressed.
No wonder so many people are stressed out to the
breaking point. No wonder the drug companies are
making billions of dollars.

Folks... no wonder our nation is in the state of
demise that we're in. This is a national tragedy.
Sound the alarm.

Not to overstate the obvious here, but... our
nation is in *big* trouble in many ways and the devil
has to be laughing at us. What a coup. Here we
are... supposedly a "Christian" nation... and the
majority of the people either don't pray at all or pray
at meals and maybe, just maybe as a last resort in
certain situations.

I wonder if our heavenly Father ever thinks...
"Will someone please *pray?*" As a matter of fact...
He has said...

> *So I sought for a man among them who*
> *would make a wall, and stand in the gap*
> *before Me on behalf of the land, that I*
> *should not destroy it; but I found no one.*

*Therefore I have poured out My indigna-
tion on them; I have consumed them with
My fire of My wrath; and I have recom-
pensed their deeds on their own heads.
(Ezekiel 22:30, 31)*

So I go back to the simple question... *do you pray?*
If the answer is "yes", then God bless you. If the
answer is "no", then my next question to you would
be... "Why not?" And if your answer is in that "yes,
at meals and holidays, and maybe when things get
really bad" category, then my response would be:

I want to encourage you... everyone... if there
was ever a time in our nation's history when people
need to be in prayer, it's now. We are at a crucial
time in the history of mankind. As people of faith...
we must pray.

Pray for the lost, the downtrodden; those who
are suffering. And pray that God, by the power of
His Holy Spirit, will have mercy on this nation of
ours. Pray for the LORD to intervene and that spiritual revival will ignite America with one more great
awakening before Jesus comes again.

My next point here is:

Who Do You Pray To?

This may sound like a dumb question... but
allow me. As politically incorrect as this is (which I
couldn't care less about), we do not all worship the
same God. My God is the God of Abraham, Isaac
and Jacob; the God of Israel; the Father of our Lord
and Savior Jesus Christ. He is the only true God
and eleven times beginning in Isaiah 43 and ending
in chapter 46, the Bible states that He alone is God

and that there is *no* other God. So, with that in mind, *if* we call ourselves Christians, we must pray to the only true God.

In addition, let me state, without purposely trying to offend anyone... nowhere in the Bible are we taught to pray to Mary. The Bible does not teach to pray to her or through her. Listen closely to this verse...

"There is one God and one Mediator between God and men, the Man Christ Jesus, who gave Himself as a ransom for all, to be testified in due time" (1 Timothy 2:5, 6).

How many Mediators? My Bible says *"one"!* Then why does anybody teach that someone would need to pray to Mary? We are not told to pray for the dead, or to the dead. This is *not* what the Scripture teaches. Remember earlier when I mentioned that we are to test the spirits by laying them down on Scripture? If something goes against the word of God, then it's wrong. The area of prayer is a great example of this. For example, nowhere are we taught in the Bible to pray rosaries. As a matter of fact the word "rosary" is nowhere in the Bible. Listen closely; 49 times in the rosary people are told to say... "Hail Mary". This is wrong; I don't know how else to say it. Was Mary blessed? Absolutely... she was the mother of our Lord and Savior. But when anyone is elevated to the status that Mary has been, it is idolatry. I say these things out of concern for a large number of people who have been deceived in this area. Be very careful about elevating Mary. I realize this is an area of controversy, but we are to expose false teachings and this is a false teaching. Someone show me the word "rosary" in the Bible. Someone show me where it says we are to pray to Mary in the Bible. It's simply not there. We are told clearly in Scripture that we are only to worship God...

> *Now I, John, saw and heard these things. And when I heard and saw, I fell down to worship before the feet of the angel who showed me these things. Then he said to me, "See that you do not do that. For I am your fellow servant, and of your brethren the prophets, and of those who keep the words of this book. Worship God." (Revelation 22:8, 9)*

Scripture is clear. We are to worship God alone... and we are instructed to pray in Jesus's name...

> *"And whatever you ask in My name, that I will do, that the Father may be glorified in the Son. If you ask anything in My name, I will do it" (John 14:13, 14).*

So... let me be clear; we are instructed to pray to the Father, in Jesus's name. It's really simple. God wants to bless our prayer life... but He wants us to pray to Him and Jesus is the only Mediator that we need. Anything more than that is not Scriptural.

My next point here is:

Are you specific when you pray?

When we pray, is it in just in general, or do we get specific? It honors God when we are specific;

let me tell you why. When you or I petition the LORD in a specific manner and then that request is granted, He receives glory and honor. In addition to that, it also builds our faith. Let me paint a picture here. Your child asks you for a great Christmas. What exactly does that mean? How do you gauge whether or not it's a great Christmas? But, if your child asks for a green bicycle and that's what they get, you know and they know that they got what they requested. They know that you answered their specific request, because you care for them and love them. We are told in the Scripture to be specific in our prayers...

> *"Be anxious for nothing, but in every-thing by prayer and supplication, with thanksgiving, let your requests be made known to God" (Philippians 4:6).*

When our prayers are very general, we may not comprehend when it's God. I want to encourage you to be specific in your prayer life. And if you can journal your prayers and thoughts, you will be amazed when you go back and see God's hand-writing on your life.

Being specific like this brings me to my next point about our prayer life...

Are you willing to pray God's will?

Many times in prison inmates ask me to pray for them. I welcome this opportunity. When they ask me to pray, often times it's for their early release. I ask them this: "Are you ready to trust the Lord?" They'll usually say "Yes, I am" and I tell them that's good, because it may be God's will to *not* give them early release, "so let's pray for His will to be done." Obviously, I get some strange looks. But, let me ask a question. What if God said... "I'm not done yet. I have you here for My purpose; I'm doing a work in you and your early release would be the worst thing for you right now because you're not ready for that yet."

Allow me to apply that same thought to all of us. What if the very thing we're praying for is *not* God's will for us? Are we willing to trust God? Are we willing to humbly submit to His authority in our life? Let me share two Scriptures with you that will help...

> *"Now this is the confidence that we have in Him. That if we ask anything according to His will, He hears us. And if we know that He hears us, whatever we ask, we know that we have the petitions that we have asked of Him"* (1 John 5:14, 15).

Notice... "according to His will" ...sometimes this is hard for us. We want our will to be His will. But we've got it backwards... we should want His will to be our will. I've heard people say... "Why won't God answer my prayer?" Maybe what we've prayed for isn't His will. Maybe He's actually protecting us by *not* giving us what we prayed for. It goes back to that trust thing. As His children, we must trust that He has our best in mind and wait for that.

Then I've also heard people say... "Doesn't it say He will give us the desires of our heart?" Yes, the Bible says that... but, let's look at that entire verse...

"Delight yourself also in the LORD and He shall give you the desires of your heart" (Psalm 37:5).

I love this verse! But notice... it says "Delight yourself in the LORD." When we begin to delight ourselves in the LORD and the things of the LORD, He begins to change our desires to His desires. The things that are important to God become important to us. And then He gives us the desires of our heart. This also is part of the transformation process that I talk about. Things that used to be important to me no longer have any value and things that once weren't important to me, now have great value in my life. This is what the Scripture means that says...

"Seek first the Kingdom of God and His righteousness, and all these things shall be added to you" (Matthew 6:33).

He wants us to seek Him and trust Him and then He will change us and transform us and meet all our needs.

I want to go back to what I mentioned at the start of the chapter... what a privilege we have in being able to pray to our Father in heaven. I am so humbled when I really meditate on the concept of prayer.

Let me make one more point about prayer to consider...

Do you want to have an effective prayer life?

Let me explain what I mean by this question. I stated earlier that as we come to a deeper understanding of prayer, it should revolutionize our lives. If we really are able to grasp the wonder of prayer, the power involved with prayer and who it is we're praying to, then we should pray about everything.

If we knew that when we pray, circumstances would change, healing would take place, lives would change, governments would rise and fall, souls would be saved and the destiny of entire nations would be altered, would that change our prayer lives? Well... Scripture says that's exactly what can happen.

I can only speak for myself, but I can tell you that I want an effective prayer life! I want to know that when I pray according to God's will, things will happen. Can I be that bold? Scripture says yes...

> *Jesus answered and said to them, "Have faith in God. For assuredly, I say to you, whoever says to this mountain, 'Be removed and be cast into the sea,' and does not doubt in his heart, but believes that those things he says will be done, he will have whatever he says. Therefore I say to you, whatever things you ask when you pray, believe that you receive them and you will have them. (Mark 11:22-24)*

These are amazing verses spoken by our Lord. If we are to be obedient to Scripture, we're told by Jesus to *believe we will receive.* Now, I'm not attempting to be a "name it and claim it" person here, but it sounds to me as though Jesus is telling us to have faith and believe we will receive when we pray. I think God loves it when His kids start to really step out and believe what His word says. Let's look at another verse...

"Without faith it is impossible to please Him, for he who comes to God must believe that He is, and that He is a rewarder of those who diligently seek Him" (Hebrews 11:6).

Excuse me, but I think God is telling us here that "if" we diligently seek Him, He will reward us. I remember the first time I saw this verse, I thought... "shouldn't have told *me* this" ...I want to seek Him diligently! I don't know about you... but this verse gets me excited. Now, what if we apply this verse to our prayer life? The Lord is telling us that we *must* believe Him. Listen to this verse...

The prayer of faith will save the sick, and the Lord will raise him up. And if he has committed sins, he will be forgiven. Confess your trespasses to one another, and pray for one another that you may be healed. The effective fervent prayer of a righteous man avails much. Elijah was a man with a nature like ours, and he prayed earnestly that it would not rain; and it did not rain on the land for three years and six months. And he prayed again, and the heaven gave rain, and the earth produced fruit. (James 5:15-18)

When we pray and believe and expect God to move onto the scene, it honors God. I believe that many times God is ready and willing to move on our behalf, if we would just ask. One of my favorite verses in the Bible is...

"For the eyes of the LORD run to and fro throughout the whole earth, to show Himself strong on behalf of those whose hearts are loyal to Him" (2 Chronicles 16:9).

God is looking for someone to show Himself strong on their behalf. I love this verse.

As I continue to grow in my walk with the Lord, I'm amazed at His grace, His love and how He seeks His kids. What an honor to be called a child of God. The reality that our Father, the creator of the universe, cares about the day to day activities in our lives and that we can pray to Him about everything; even now when I think about it almost brings me to tears.

As I conclude this chapter I would like to encourage you to pray and ask the Holy Spirit to give you a fresh perspective about your prayer life. I know this sounds odd, but let's pray for the Lord to bless our prayer lives...

"Lord, what an amazing privilege we have as Your children to come to You and pour out our hearts to You. As we express our concerns, anxieties, joys and requests; we ask that You would bless our prayer lives. Help us to pray Your desires and help us to pray Your will. Lord, use our prayers for Your kingdom purposes. When we don't know what we should pray for, send Your Holy Spirit to help us in our weakness. Give us a deeper understanding of You and a deeper appreciation for the honor of praying to You. Father, help us with our unbelief.

Strengthen us in our prayers and help us grow in our faith. Thank You for Your patience, Your goodness, Your grace and mercy. Thank You, Lord for hearing our prayers. In Jesus's name... Amen!"

Chapter 16

It's Time to Take a Stand

—⚶—

There is a saying that goes like this...
"If you're not willing to stand for something, you'll fall for anything."

I mentioned earlier in the book that I am a Type A personality. I'm sure in reading this far you've had no problem picking up on this fact as well. I remember one time my dad told me that if I wasn't careful my mouth would end up getting me in trouble. That has been a true statement on more than one occasion.

However, there's a flip side to that. God made me the way He made me, just as He has done with all of His kids. As the Potter, when God prepares His vessels, He then begins to use them. What an honor it is to be evangelist, a witness and a spokesperson for the Kingdom of my Father in heaven. My prayer is that He will continue to use my mouth for His purposes.

I also mentioned earlier that God has given me a "watchman" calling. Allow me to explain...

I gave the Scripture in an earlier chapter, but let's look at it again...

Son of man, I have made you a watchman for the house of Israel; therefore hear a word from My mouth, and give them a warning from Me: When I say to the wicked, "You shall surely die," and you give him no warning, nor speak to warn the wicked from his wicked way, to save his life, that same wicked man shall die in his iniquity; but his blood I will require at your hand.

Yet, if you warn the wicked, and he does not turn from his wickedness, nor from his wicked way, he shall die in his iniquity; but you have delivered your soul... But when I speak with you, I will open your mouth, and you shall say to them, "Thus says the Lord God." He who hears, let him hear and he who refuses, let him refuse; for they are a rebellious house. (Ezekiel 3:17-19, 27)

These are some very powerful words from the Lord. The first time that I read them, I was stunned. I almost wish sometimes that I wouldn't have read them. I knew as soon as I read them that the Lord was speaking to me. I have mentioned that I love the word of God. As strange as this may sound... I love these types of verses just like I love the verses on prosperity and peace and love.

The word of God is amazing... just as it will comfort us and encourage us, it will also correct us and show us our faults. Whether it be on a personal level or for a nation, God's word is the final authority. When God says something, He means what He says...

"God is not a man, that He should lie, nor a son of man, that He should repent. Has He said, and will He not do? Or has He spoken, and will He not make it good?" (Numbers 23:19).

God doesn't have to apologize to anyone for anything. All His judgments are righteous. He is the final authority in *all* matters. And His word is true. It was true when it was written; and it is still true today. Whether you or I agree with God's word has no bearing on His word. Proverbs says...

"There is a way that seems right to a man, but its end is the way of death" (Proverbs 14:12).

This verse applies to us as individuals and it also applies to us as a nation. I don't know how else to state this, so I will just say it...

America, as a nation, is in very deep trouble!

We as a nation are at a crossroads. When I hear people talk about America, I hear so many different things. But what I don't hear people say very often is what I think is glaringly obvious.

We as a nation have turned from the Lord. One of my best friends in this world is a man named Jeremy. He points out to me that there are still many solid Christians out there in America and I thank God for that. But with that in mind, here is my question:

With so many solid Christians out there, why is America at the place we're at? Why are we as a nation thumbing our nose at God's word? The leaders are elected officials that represent the people and yet the decisions and laws that are being put in place in our country today are taking us down a road that will destroy us as a nation. And the signs are everywhere. And yet so many of us go to church... we go to ballgames with the kids and grandkids... we go to work week in and week out... we may even be involved in a Bible study once a week... but we continue to slide down a slippery slope that will ultimately destroy us as a great nation. And to a large part... the church in America has grown silent. Listen to these verses and allow them to sink in... then apply them to us as a nation...

> *Do this, knowing the time, that now it is high time to awake out of sleep; for now our salvation is nearer than when we first believed. The night is far spent, the day is at hand. Therefore let us cast off the works of darkness, and let us put on the armor of light. Let us walk properly, as in the day, not in revelry and drunkenness, not in lewdness and lust, not in strife and envy. But put on the Lord Jesus Christ, and make no provision for the flesh, to fulfill its lust. (Romans 13:11-14)*

These words were written by the Apostle Paul, but I challenge you that they are so very relevant for our nation today. The church in America has fallen asleep and it is high time for the church to awake out of sleep. What many people fail to grasp, including many of the solid Christian people that my friend Jeremy speaks about, is this...

We are in a spiritual battle for the very fabric and life of our nation! Let me ask everyone reading this a question: if we were attacked as a nation here at home, if we were invaded right now by enemy forces and they began killing our friends and families across America, wouldn't we take up arms and defend ourselves? Well...I'm here to sound the alarm! We are under attack. The enemy is Satan and he has invaded our nation. And he is more powerful and destructive then any enemy we have ever faced before. And he is here right now... he snuck in under the cover of night... and he is systematically destroying us.

America is under attack in the following areas:

- Marriage between one man and one woman
- The family structure as we know it
- The church
- The youth in our nation
- The word of God
- The Christian foundations and values of our nation

This is why it is high time for *all* Christians to awake out of sleep. The greatest threat to America is not terrorism, although that *is* a real threat. The greatest threat to America is not our debt, although that *is* a real threat. The greatest threat to America is not foreign enemies, although that is a real threat. The greatest threat to America *is* that we are literally rotting from the inside out, both morally and spiritually!

Listen closely to these verses from Jeremiah and apply them to America...

The Lord is speaking here...

"I brought you into a bountiful country, to eat its fruit and its goodness. But when you entered, you defiled My land and made My heritage an abomination. The priests did not say, "Where is the LORD?" And those who handle the law did not know Me; the rulers also transgressed against Me; the prophets prophesied by Baal, and walked after things that do not profit... Has a nation changed its gods, which are not gods? But My people have changed their Glory for what does not profit.

Be astonished, O heavens, at this, and be horribly afraid; for My people have committed two evils; they have forsaken Me, the fountain of living waters, and hewn themselves cisterns – broken cisterns that can hold no water... Your own wickedness will correct you, and your backslidings will rebuke you. Know therefore and see that it is an evil and bitter thing that you have forsaken the LORD your God, and the fear of Me is not in you," says the Lord God of hosts. (Jeremiah 2:7, 8, 11-13, 19)

I was speaking at a men's breakfast a few years ago and as I sat at the table eating with an older gentleman, I asked him for some wisdom and to speak to me about what he thought was wrong with America. He made one statement that has stuck with me since then... he said, "We've lost the fear of the Lord in America." I couldn't agree with him more. Notice that at the end of these verses from Jeremiah, that's exactly what God says: "the fear of Me is not in you."

That word "fear" in the original Hebrew language means "reverential awe", "respect with obedience", "in humble submission to", but it also means "Godly fear". We *have* lost the "fear of the Lord" in this nation.

Someone may say, "Craig, that's not very loving. God is love and He doesn't want us to fear Him." Well, Jesus was speaking about the fact that the world hated Him and they would hate us as well and then He spoke these words about who we should fear...

> *"Whatever I tell you in the dark, speak in the light; and what you hear in the ear, preach on the housetops. And do not fear those who kill the body but cannot kill the soul. But rather fear Him who is able to destroy both soul and body in hell"* (Matthew 10:27, 28).

And yet... we have come to the place where we fear man more than we do God. We seek the approval of society more than we seek to please God.

When did we adopt the phrase "politically correct" and why is it so important? When did the voices of a few people that live their lives with no restraint become the law of the land? How did we get to the place in America where we believe that we know what's right and wrong, even when it goes directly against what God says?

Most of us remember growing up and at some point we got into trouble for something and our response was... "Well, Jimmy was doing it..." or, "Everybody else was doing it" and usually one of our parents would respond back... "Does that mean if Jimmy was going to jump off a building you'd do it?" Well... I want to ask the same thing now... just because so many others are going down the wrong path... does that mean we *all* are supposed to?

I used to wonder about a set of verses that Jesus spoke... but now these verses have become crystal clear to me. Listen to what Jesus said...

> *"Enter by the narrow gate; for wide is the gate and broad is the way that leads to destruction, and there are many who go in by it. How narrow is the gate and difficult is the way that leads to life, and there are few who find it" (Matthew 7:13, 14).*

The reason I used to wonder about these verses is because the majority of people in America say that they're saved. But that's not what Jesus said... He said that the majority of people are going down the wrong road... the road to destruction. By the way... that word "destruction" in the original Greek is *apoleia* and it means "damnation". So Jesus is saying here that "broad is the way that leads to damnation and there are many who go in by it."

There are many who think this kind of talk is hate speech, but it's not hate speech; it's the truth. Jesus said it... so that settles it. If this offends people, He said it would.

Allow me to ask a question here: would you rather be "politically correct" and be on the road to destruction that Jesus talked about, or would you rather surrender your life to Jesus as Lord, take a stand for the truth of Scripture and be on that road to eternal life that Jesus said few would find?

The reason that these verses are crystal clear to me now is because we as a nation are exactly what Jesus was talking about. There are so many that are on that road to destruction and it seems that the narrow road that He talked about is becoming more and more difficult, just like He said it would be. It's becoming more difficult to take a stand for the truth of God's word and not compromise to what the world says is right. But take a stand we must.

In Matthew 24, Jesus's disciples asked Him what would be the sign of His return. Jesus mentions four times in the following verses that many would be deceived. The spirit of deception is rampant in our world today. Deception is one of the main tools the devil has always used, because he's a liar. The devil knows his days are numbered and this deception will continue to get worse as we get closer to the return of Jesus Christ...

> *"All who desire to live godly in Christ Jesus will suffer persecution. But evil men and impostors will grow worse and worse, deceiving and being deceived"* *(2 Timothy 3:12, 13).*

When Micah and I first got married, we talked about the fact that as time went by, we knew that it would become more and more difficult to live for Christ and that there would possibly come a day that we would lose some friends because of our decision not to compromise our Biblical values.

There are some things that we can't be a part of... some events that we don't get invited to.

That day has come; we all are now under increased pressure to be silent about our faith. We are at the point: either take a stand for Christ and for what the Bible teaches, or to go along with what the world says is right and wrong. We all are having to make that choice now.

I've already made mine. Because of what the Lord has done in my life, this has been an easy decision for me. I choose to surrender to Jesus as my Lord and Savior and to come under the authority of Scripture as the guide for my life.

That doesn't mean I'm perfect; it means that when I stumble, I will confess my sin, repent (which means to turn from) and ask the Holy Spirit to strengthen me in that area. It means that I am forgiven. But it also means that I am to contend earnestly for the faith. It means that I am to be a witness for Jesus Christ. And it means that I am to have no fellowship with the works of darkness, but rather expose them. It means all of these things because that's what the Bible says it means.

It's time to wake up, America!

I said at the start of this chapter that there's a saying:

"If you're not willing to stand for something, you'll fall for anything."

I've now witnessed in my own country this to be a true statement. Because we've not stood for the truth... we're falling for anything. How far down this road of perversion and decadence will we go? At this time, no one can say for sure.

What I can say for sure is this: if we in America who call ourselves by the name of Christ choose to remain silent at this time in our nation's history... if we're not willing to stand up and speak out... and if we allow people who are rebellious to God's word to lead us in the direction that we're currently headed, then America as we know it will come to an end.

Does that startle you? It needs to... Think about this... if God would allow America to rebel against Him and His word without any correction and ultimately without judgment... then He would have to go back and apologize to Sodom and Gomorrah...

> *"Sodom and Gomorrah, and the cities around them in a similar manner to these, having given themselves over to sexual immorality and gone after strange flesh, are set forth as an example, suffering the vengeance of eternal fire" (Jude 7).*

The phrase there... "given themselves over to sexual immorality and gone after strange flesh" is exactly what I'm talking about when I mention being "politically correct". The sexual immorality that is such a divisive topic in our nation today is homosexuality. We are now being told that we should accept this type of behavior. However, God's word is absolutely clear on the topic of homosexuality... it is sexual immorality and it is sin. And the Scripture here says that Sodom and Gomorrah were left "as an example". That means we should observe and learn from. I understand that this is not a popular viewpoint to take a stand for. But if God says that we will be destroyed if we do these things... shouldn't we make every effort to expose them and bring them into the light of Scripture?

This is what I mean when I say that being a watchman is not a very popular role. But the role of a watchman is to give a warning... and that's my intention here... to give a warning...

> *For you were once darkness, but now you are light in the Lord. Walk as children of light (for the fruit of the Spirit is in all goodness, righteousness, and truth), finding out what is acceptable to the Lord. And have no fellowship with the unfruitful works of darkness, but rather expose them. (Ephesians 5:8-11)*

As Christians... we are called to "expose the works of darkness". It takes courage to speak up in a loving way... but God's word is clear about this. In the future it will become increasingly difficult to take a stand for truth... the Bible teaches that this world will continue to get worse, not better.

We must settle our minds, that despite the loud voices who will persecute those of us who stand for the truth... we must stand... and with as much love as we can, we must be willing to speak up... before it's too late.

I understand that defending the faith and defending the truth of Scripture *is* not and *will* not be easy. I also understand that things will continue to get worse... but I want to encourage everyone who calls themselves a follower of Jesus Christ...

It's Time to Take a Stand!

This is when the Holy Spirit will strengthen us and will speak through us to a dying world. Obedience to the Lord is not always easy. We should pray for one another that we will be the light in the darkness that God wants us to be.

"Father, You alone are sovereign. You alone know the end from the beginning. You have blessed America in so many ways and we as a nation have turned from You. We have sinned against You in not taking heed according to Your word. We have become a rebellious nation that thinks we know better than You what is right and wrong. We have allowed the enemy to lead us in paths that will not profit us. LORD, we ask that You have mercy on us and forgive us not because of who we are, but because of who You are. For those of us who are called by Your name, strengthen us and give us the courage to speak as we ought to speak. Help us to discern between good and evil and then raise us up to be the salt and light that You've called us to be in this nation. We seek Your forgiveness. We seek Your mercy. We ask that You pour out Your Holy Spirit upon this nation, that You would cleanse us, purify us and continue to shine Your light through us unto a dark world that so desperately needs Jesus Christ. And finally Father, we ask that Your Kingdom come on earth as it is in heaven. We ask these things... in Jesus's name. Amen."

Chapter 17

Urgency!

—⁓—

This book has been about my journey with Jesus. If there is one thing that I would like people to take away from reading this book it's this:

No matter what you've done in your life... or what someone that you may know has done in their life... don't lose hope; it's not too late! If Jesus changed my life, he *can* and *will* change anyone's life. That's what He does... He changes lives!

I pray that by reading this book, the transforming power of God has been revealed. I love the picture that our Father in heaven is the Potter, we are the clay and that He is in the process of reshaping each of us into a vessel that can be useful to the Potter.

We are all different from one another and we have different gifts. You may be called to be a missionary in a foreign land. Or you may be gifted with a healing ministry. You may be called to care for the elderly, or to teach in a children's ministry. One of the awesome things about the Lord is that because He made us; He knows exactly what our gifts and callings are. If you want to know what your gifts are... just ask...

"Every good gift and every perfect gift is from above and comes down from the Father of lights" (James 1:17).

We are living in very serious times... we need the Holy Spirit to be able to discern between good and evil and to live a victorious life in Christ. If you've never asked to be filled with the Holy Spirit; you can do that in a very simple way... just ask... here's how Jesus put it...

So I say to you, ask, and it will be given to you; seek, and you will find; knock, and it will be opened to you. For everyone who asks receives, and he who seeks finds, and to him who knocks it will be opened. If a son asks for bread from any father among you, will he give him a stone? Or if he asks for a fish, will he give him a serpent instead of a fish? Or if he asks for an egg, will he offer him a scorpion? If you then, being evil, know how to give good gifts to your children, how much more will your heavenly Father give the Holy Spirit to those who ask Him! (Luke 11:9-13)

I remember the first time I stopped and meditated on these verses... so... you're telling me that I can just ask for the Holy Spirit and God will give Him to me? Read it again... that's what Jesus said. So... if you've never asked for the Holy Spirit... you can do it now.

Just get quiet... get still... and ask the LORD for the Holy Spirit.

This is very, very important... please, if you've never done this... I want to encourage you.

One of the main reasons we need the Holy Spirit is because He dwells within us. He is our Guide to righteous living. He is also our teacher. Without the help of the Holy Spirit, we're not able to understand the deep things of God, the deep truths of Scripture...

> *"But the Helper, the Holy Spirit, whom the Father will send in My name, He will teach you all things, and bring to your remembrance all things that I said to you" (John 14:26).*

This is one of my favorite verses in Scripture. As I was locked behind the prison walls, I was alone with the Holy Spirit as my teacher. Even now when I study, I always ask the Holy Spirit to teach me what He wants me to know about God's word. Listen to how Paul explained this...

> *These things we also speak, not in words which man's wisdom teaches but which the Holy Spirit teaches, comparing spiritual things with spiritual. But the natural man does not receive the things of the Spirit of God, for they are foolishness to him; nor can he know them, because they are spiritually discerned. But he who is spiritual judges all things, yet he himself is rightly judged by no one. For who has known the mind of the LORD that he may instruct Him? But we have the mind of Christ. (1 Corinthians 2:13-16)*

These are some deep verses, but we can see here that the Holy Spirit is the One who teaches about the spiritual things that we need to learn.

He is also where we receive the power that is needed to live in these last days before Christ returns. To be witnesses for Jesus and to stand against the lies of the enemy, we need the power of the Holy Spirit. Jesus told His disciples just before He ascended into heaven...

"But you shall receive power when the Holy Spirit has come upon you; and you shall be witnesses to Me in Jerusalem, and in all Judea and Samaria, and to the end of the earth" (Acts 1:8).

As I mentioned, there are different gifts that we have. The Holy Spirit also empowers us to use those gifts for Kingdom purposes. What I want to do in this final chapter is to encourage others to use their gifts, whatever those gifts may be. Why would anybody have a gift from God and not want to use it?

I know that my gifts include being an evangelist and also teaching the word of God. Both of these come very easy to me and I love to do both. That's one of the ways we can tell what our gifts are. The Lord usually won't call us to something that we hate to do. There may be assignments that He calls us to do that we're not comfortable with, or we don't feel as though we will be able to succeed at, but if He calls us to a task, He will equip us to accomplish that task.

Through my journey... the Holy Spirit has revealed my gifts to me and then He has ignited a fire in me. There is a burning inside of me, an urgency to tell others about Jesus Christ. Anybody that meets me learns within a few minutes that I love the Lord and that He changed my life.

Now, to the title of this final chapter...

Urgency!

Let me give you something to think about... let's suppose that we are living in the last days. While the Bible teaches that no one knows the day or the hour, it also teaches that we can discern the time. And the signs that need to take place before Jesus returns have occurred. So, if we *are* living in the last days (however short of time that may be) shouldn't that create in us urgency?

We should be serious about our prayer life; we should live our lives in a way that witnesses to others and brings glory to God and we should be looking for the soon return of Jesus Christ.

Allow me to give you a few Scriptures to meditate on in the closing of this book...

> *"The end of all things is at hand; therefore be serious and watchful in your prayers"* (1 Peter 4:7).

That word "hand" means "drawing very near" in the Greek. This verse has urgency to it. Peter is telling us to be sober minded; to be observant and watchful of things going on around us. The word "end" means "the conclusion" and the word "things" means "whole" or "everything". This is a warning verse from Peter that this whole world as we know it *will* come to an end. As people of Christ, we are called here to be serious about our prayers. We should be praying for each other, for our nation, and for the nation of Israel. That's right... we are told to pray for Israel...

"Pray for the peace of Jerusalem"
(Psalm 122:6).

We are also called to be serious about our behavior. I know that people watch my day to day walk. They are watching yours, too. The greatest witness tool we have is our daily life...

"For God did not call us to unclean-
ness, but to holiness. Therefore he who
rejects this does not reject man, but God,
who has also given us His Holy Spirit"
(1 Thessalonians 4:7, 8).

I know that the unbelieving world watches those of us who call ourselves "Christian" to see how we live our daily lives. We are called to be different. That might make some people uncomfortable... but the word of God teaches that we're not to be the same as the rest of the world. I mentioned these verses earlier, but I want to look at them again here...

Do not be unequally yoked with unbe-
lievers. For what fellowship has righ-
teousness with lawlessness? And what
communion has light with darkness?
And what accord has Christ with Belial?
Or what part has a believer with an
unbeliever? And what agreement has
the temple of God with idols? For you

are the temple of the living God. As God has said: "I will dwell in them and walk among them. I will be their God, and they shall be My people."

Therefore "Come out from among them and be separate," says the Lord. "Do not touch what is unclean, and I will receive you. I will be a Father to you, and you shall be My sons and daughters," says the LORD Almighty. Therefore, having these promises, beloved, let us cleanse ourselves from all filthiness of the flesh and spirit, perfecting holiness in the fear of God. (2 Corinthians 6:14-7:1)

Allow me to make a point here: as I sit and type these verses... I have to tell you that I am flooded with gratitude for His mercy and His grace. While I am called to be different from the world, I still miss the mark so many times. I live in the world and my flesh still rears its ugly head... and I fall short. So... thank God that He is patient with me. Thank God that He doesn't give me what I deserve. Because if I got what I deserved... I would burn in hell.

This book is about the goodness of God... that He looked down from His throne and that He could love someone like me enough to say to His Son... "Go down there and provide a way for people like Craig... go down there and be the perfect sacrifice for these people... that they will be My sons and daughters, too."

This book is about how God, in His mercy and grace, will take someone like me and change their eternal destiny. And that He will transform us from what we were... into what He wants us to be... I am *so* far from what I will be... He's not done yet. I still need so much polishing... so much smoothing. And by His grace, the Potter will continue the good work that He's begun in me.

Because of His love for me, I am compelled to tell other people about Him. Because I know personally of His goodness, I must be a witness for Him. I am a witness that the goodness of God leads us to repentance. I am a sinner that needs a savior. Left to my own I'm in trouble. So... I've put my trust and my faith in one greater than me... I've put my trust and my faith in Jesus Christ. He's my Lord... He's my Savior. He's the One who died for me and took the punishment that I deserved, but that I couldn't take. Thanks be to God Almighty for sending His Son for people like me.

There are still many people who need to hear about the love of Jesus Christ. There are many people who are hurting... who are suffering... who are lost and are wandering in the world. And time is short. We really are nearer than when we first believed. So there is urgency! We whose names are written in the Lamb's Book of Life must tell others about the saving grace of God before it's too late.

I hope that this book has been a blessing in some ways to you who have taken the time to read it. Thank you for taking time from your life to listen to my story. If this book has helped you in any way to either surrender your life to Christ or has helped you in your journey with the Lord, then it has accomplished what I started out for it to accomplish.

Will you do me a favor? Pass the book along to someone else that you think it might help, or get a few copies and give them to people who you think of. And will you please pray that God will continue to use my life for His Kingdom purposes.

"Father, I pray that You would bless those who have read this book. And that this book would be an instrument that You would use to open blind eyes, and free the captives from the chains of the enemy. And Lord... let Your Kingdom come on earth as it is in heaven... in Jesus's precious name, amen!"

Come Jesus, come... come soon!

May the peace of the Lord be upon you and keep you... God bless you...

Craig Nedrow

B

Ned 246

Nedrow, Craig

Free indeed: From prison to prosperity

B
N
F

DATE	ISSUED TO

DATE DUE

CPSIA information can be obtained at www.ICGtesting.com
Printed in the USA
LVOW08s2042120713

342523LV00003B/4/P